me of Passenger Chick

m Pers Frost

NY, United States

ght 23 Seat 14C

le _____ Gate B14

Speaking Our Truths:
Celebrating our
Stories
Voices of Brooklyn
Generation

CONTENTS

Your Story is also amazing
And your voice is matter [handwritten signature]

Strive to be better [handwritten, signed KH]
Adventures are the best story [handwritten]
Be You Stay You !! S.S [handwritten]
Thank You for Your Support [handwritten signature]

your voice matters so tell your story Victor

Forget your past, not the lessons you learn
Bul

FOREWARD

This book truly embodies the fabric of America. It features stories of hope, fear and dreams. This book serves as a reminder that our most positive asset is to build the confidence of our young people. The College Prep Academy at Brooklyn Generation High School became the lab, a safe space for thoughtfulness, and the environment that allowed ingenuity to breathe.

It was early in the summer of 2017 when I first heard their stories. The classroom was filled with bright eyed students dressed in their neatly ironed Youth Leader Shirts as their coaches and fearless advocates, Ms. Dunham and Mrs. Hill, reminded them that all things are possible. It was only a thought held by a few passionate students, that they too could write a book and tell their stories... expressing their deepest fears, their burning passions, and their hopes that one day life will grant them a slice of good measure... SUCCESS!

This book exhales hope and stands as a testimony that all things are indeed possible. It opens the door for other students to express themselves and understand that failure is not an option. The stories are real and pointed. This book answers the questions of whether our children can write their own books and tell their own stories. It is a must-read for parents, a must-have for teenagers and guide for practitioners. Young people are dreamers with faith and doubts... they were not born broken. These are extraordinary stories from future leaders, speaking their truths and celebrating their stories.

Dr. Cecil Wright

The Brooklyn Generation School College Prep Academy Youth Leaders would like to thank the many people who helped bring our words into the world:

Dana Aloisio

Octavia James

Marcy Wehling

Anna Wolk

Dr. Cecil Wright

Robin Simmons

Urban Arts Partnership: including Chris Tunkel, Aminah Abusway, Kelli Dunham

Each One Reach One/ Ms. Michele Hill

Patrick Fernbach and RowNYC

Mohamed Kaba, Brooklyn College Trio

Maria Luisa Tucker

Administration of BGS including Ms. LC and Louis Garcia

Octavia Leona Kohner & Tom Leger

Andre J. Utley, Photographer (XTRAPOSURE.COM)

And all the other people I'm forgetting!

Are you a middle schooler or a middle school parent looking for a high school that values YOUR VOICE? Join us at Brooklyn Generation. We're small in size so we're like a family but we've got lots of heart. As a NYC Community School, we offer many unique opportunities through our academic partnerships with the Arthur Ashe Institute for Urban Health, the Science Technology Entry Program at Long Island University, the Foundation for the Revival of Classical Music, College Now and Brooklyn College and Brooklyn College TRIO.

Our lead community based organization, Urban Arts Partnership, provides us with drumming, dancing, step, Story Studio, success mentoring, talent shows, and much more.

Join us and maybe you can be a part of the next VOICES OF BGS book! 718-968-4200

High School Code: L32A.

ROSE LANDA SOLON

I AM WISE AND LOVELY

I am wise and lovely:
I wonder who I am sometimes,
I hear the voice of my best friend,
I see the presence of Lord at my side,
I want to become a poet.

I am wise and lovely:
I pretend that I'm a princess,
I feel like a butterfly,
I touch my pen everyday,
I worry about people who suffer,
I cry when I can't help people who need help.

I am wise and lovely:
I understand all humans,
I dream of becoming a doctor,
I try to do my best to make all the thing possible.

I am wise and lovely.

A DAY OF DESTRUCTION IN MY COUNTRY: HAITI, JANUARY 12, 2010

An introduction: before I start telling you this story let me introduce myself. My name is Rose Landa Solon. I'm friendly, wise, and lovely, my favorite color is pink, and soccer is my favorite sport. My passion is poetry. I have written many poems but they are in other languages (Creole and French). My poems are mostly about love, but I write about different types of love: family, friend, and romantic love.

I would like to talk about the catastrophic event that lies in the memories of me, my family, and all Haitian people.

It was a Tuesday afternoon. A big catastrophic event occurred in my country, Haiti. That day marked a horror, not just for myself but all the Haitian people, even those who didn't live in Haiti.

All of us were impacted by that catastrophe but each of us were affected in different ways.

So many were dead, so many were wounded, and more became homeless. Those who were didn't have these type of things happen, lost people in their families. All of us were impacted, all of the Haitian people were in pain.

I can't forget this: people who didn't die went to pick up the bodies of their loved ones. They weren't able to find them because there were so many bodies in the street. Everywhere. People started to get diseases from the bodies. This was the worst. They didn't really have money to go to hospital because they lost everything that they had.

This devastating catastrophic event I'm talking about was an earthquake that devastated my country and left over 200,000 people dead and 895,000 homeless. Cholera, fever, and malnutrition increased as did disease. Access to education, hospitals, and food decreased.

I had heard talk of earthquakes. In school, from my parents. But January, 12 2010 was my first experience in an earthquake. I heard that many students were trapped under the rubbish when their school collapsed.

I remember during the earthquake that my aunt came rushing to my house, asking for a white blanket to cover her dead daughter who had died due to being trapped under fallen rocks.

A lot of people lost their limbs after the earthquake, which in some cases was unnecessary. This practice could have been prevented by making good medical judgement rather them medical emotion. This type of injustice is very unfortunate and very painful. There were many unreported deaths and serious injuries that were untreated secondary to lack of medical resources and treatment unavailable to the vast majorities of the poor residing in many vicinities of the country.

Although many countries tried to help Haiti after the earthquake, it wasn't enough because there was very little access to the majority of the people. There was not enough effort put into reaching the mass population, especially the poor. According to many reports, many children became orphans and some were taken advantage of by people who called themselves helpers. They said they were giving them shelter by adopting them, and instead they exploited the children.

I'd also like to talk about how, out of the money that was collected for reconstruction of Haiti, very little was used to rebuild. The majority of the money was stolen by the government for their personal use and gain, and it was used to buy big homes and finance expensive trips. They enjoyed all the wealth at the expense of the people. The poor were left in the street with horrendous conditions, and no access to medical care or facilities to get treatment for the injuries. They were left hungry, suffering with no food, no money, no place to call home, no electricity, and no clean water.

Many conflicting opinions have emerged in the wake of the earthquake. Some people state that Haitians practice so-called black magic, therefore the earthquake was a punishment from God. I firmly believe it was a wake-up call from God to tell the world to get along: stop killing each other, and stop doing evil to other people. We have to put our hands together to help each other.

Eight years after this catastrophic event, a lot of people are still displaced and living on the street with nothing. I sometimes wonder why this is happening to them after eight years. I don't have an answer, only the government can answer that. And others, like the Clintons, the Red Cross, and other organizations who donated to Haiti to help victims rebuild.

After all this time, nothing much as has been done for the mass population, and this is insufficient.

DANIEL LEWIS

AS TOLD TO SHERELL HENRY

WINGS TO FLY

My life so far can be summarized into one simple sentence: "Memories which depict a picture, that I have no words for." Everyone has a past, which creates the person we later become, whether that past caused us to sob or feel exceptionally happy.

I was born and raised in Kingston, Jamaica until I was about 10 years old. I loved living in Jamaica more than living in the U.S. Something about the hot, humid climate makes me fall in love with my home country each time I return. It wasn't just that Jamaica was warm and beautiful, but I felt emotionally safer there as well. Back home, my friends and classmates were a form of another family, one that was comforting and safe.

Moving to the U.S. wasn't much of a choice. My mother simply told me I was going to live with my father. I wouldn't say I was completely shocked, but I was surprised and even speechless at first. Now that I'm older I understand how much my mother wanted me to have an education and a future, something that was not available to me in Jamaica. It was an adjustment knowing that I was going to spend the rest of my life with a person I didn't know well.

When I first migrated to the U.S. I lived with my father. At that time, our relationship was not great. In fact, I didn't even know him very well. My father was not the type to embrace his children. He's stern and aggressive. Added to that, my step-mother had seven kids, four of whom lived with my father and me. They weren't all nice. With all of us together living under one roof it still sometimes didn't feel like a family; we did not consider each other a family. My step-mother and I never agreed or got along. Watching us interact would be like watching an episode of Tom and Jerry. I was Jerry, continuously running to save my life but also outsmarting Tom. My step-mother was like Tom and I tried my best to live cautiously with her. After disagreements with my step-mother, my father would beat me. Yes, I cried, but after this there wasn't much that I could do besides put a smile on my face to protect myself.

One day I went to school and my teacher happened to see the marks upon my skin. She asked how I got them. After this, I was sent to see a doctor and I was brought to a police station. After waiting a long time I was told I was going to foster care. The clothes on my back and the books in my bag is what I had when I ended up in the foster care system.

I had been out of school for about two weeks. They placed me with Ms. Walker, my foster mother. She is the sweetest woman I met, ever. Though she wasn't my birth mother, I loved her just as much as if she were. I enjoyed living with her; she made sure I was safe and had what I needed and sometimes even what I wanted. As a child I did sports and went to therapy. Though I was smart but made stupid mistakes, my foster mother treated me well because she saw the potential I carried within me. I played soccer and was extremely close with my foster brother. I enjoyed being in foster care because it felt like a family. I felt more a part of a family than when I was with my dad; it felt more like a home. We had family dinners and barbeques, and over time I made more and more loving and special memories. At one point when I was speaking to my therapist I said I missed Jamaica and wanted to go back. The therapist helped make that happen. I went back to live with mother in Jamaica for a time and returned to the United States at age 15.

Coming back to the U.S., I once again had to leave my family behind and live far from my school. Every day I left my house on Staten Island by no later than 6:00 a.m. to ensure that I would arrive at Brooklyn Generation School (BGS) by 8:30 a.m. I was on the BGS track team. The practices were after school so I didn't reach home until 8:30 p.m.

I pushed through and graduated from BGS. I'm thankful for Ms Hill and the other BGS teachers who were always on my side. I am thankful to my mother who is my best friend, who has always been there when I needed her most, who has forced me out of my comfort zone, and who creating a loving home for me.

Now I attend Farmingdale College in Long Island and I am also a pilot. Although my life hasn't been an easy one, it created the man I am today, the man that I am proud of. If you learn anything from my story, learn that life will never be easy and it will never be the perfect movie. Life will push you further than you think you can go, but never give up. You have wings to fly; your success is just around the corner.

MIA LOCKHART

WHO I WAS BEFORE LIFE HAPPENED

Growing up in the Caribbean, I was known to be a very strong person: a girl who stood up for herself and was not broken by people, a girl who believed in herself no matter the odds against her, and a girl who could find the little piece of light within complete darkness. At least that's what I was, before my whole world came crashing down. At my old school, Bridgeport High, I participated in track and field. I was very good at it, so good at it that I became captain of the girl's track and field team. Not only was I a fast sprinter but I was good leader with perfect attendance, good grades, and a good example to others. My coach, Mr. Thompson, would always ask, "Are you ready for practice today?" My response never changed. "Always, Coach Thompson."

Last year my entire life was turned upside down. During the summer I gained a few pounds, my mom traveled back and forth to the U.S., and my brother was having health problems that left me with a lot of responsibility. I felt completely alone with nobody to lean on for support. When track season started I was a bit slower than I expected, and it was noticeable to everyone. At first, I tried hard to keep it from bothering me because my sight was set on one goal: to get faster than I was last year. I had trouble reaching my goal as I was continually bullied by my own teammates. These were the same teammates I called my "friends" the previous year.

"Hey Mia, why so slow? Oh that's right, you're fat!" That was one of the few jokes they made.

I never replied because it wasn't worth it to stoop so low. Replying was beneath me because I knew who I was and where I came from. The next few months went by smoothly. I thought they would just drop it or find something new to talk about, but then the name calling and the jokes went too far. I didn't want to talk to anyone about it and stress out people who had their own problems. The more these comments came at me, the more my self-confidence and self-esteem lowered. It was so bad that I even considered cutting myself just to ease the pain that I felt. Thank God I didn't do it. Instead I talked with a friend and she helped me figure out my options. Eventually I decided to give up track and field temporarily until I could get some confidence back. I just needed to concentrate on healing myself.

During the Christmas break after that semester, I went to a therapist, and got some advice and support that I needed to end the misery that I was in. By the end of the break I felt almost like myself again. "Drop those people who you call your friends, but before you do that, make amends with them. Even if they're the ones in the wrong, forgive them and then move on with your life," Ms. Dixon, my therapist, said. "Ok, I'll try my best," I said.

January 7, 2016 was the start of a whole new school year and I felt ready to stand up against my so-called friends. I let them know that I forgave them for the torment they put me through. As my disappearance from track stretched into a week, my coach cornered me in school and asked, "Why aren't you running anymore?" I told him what I went through in the previous months, and he asked, "Why didn't you come to me? I don't only think of you as a student athlete, but as a daughter I never had."

"I'm sorry I didn't tell you what my own teammates put me through, I just wanted to figure it out on my own. I also think of you as a father figure whenever I'm at school, as well as my coach," I replied.

"Come back, even if you have to practice by yourself. I will allow it," he said.

"Ok, I'll come back, and yes I would love to practice by

myself, thank you."

"You're welcome," he responded.

I restarted track and without having to practice with the bullies, I got faster and stronger than ever. Not only was I proud, but most importantly my self-confidence and self-esteem was back to where it was before, and I was happy.

> *"Bad things do happen; how [you] respond to them defines [your] character and the quality of [your] life. [You] can choose to sit in perpetual sadness, immobilized by the gravity of [your] loss, or [you] can rise from the pain and treasure the most precious gift [you] have--life itself."   -Walter Anderson*

KESTON HALL

BAD KARMA

In order to fully understand this story you have to imagine yourself as a pre-teen who doesn't know lots of things. In this story I caused a heartbreak, and then it came back to haunt me. So I'll start from the first part because, you know, chronological order. Anyway, flash back to when I was in the fourth grade. I didn't care about girls, really. All I cared about was watching the new Speed Racer episode or buying the new Hot Wheels toy car set. I'm a gearhead if you can't tell. I remember the first day I was extremely hyped to go to school and see my friends. Unfortunately it is different now.

I remember meeting this new girl, let's call her Dinah, I guess. She and I started to become friends, talking almost every day. Then she asked me something like, *Have you ever wondered what it's like to be boyfriend and girlfriend.* I said I hadn't, but then she hit me with the question, "What if we tried it out?"

As a fourth grader, I wasn't ready for a relationship, of course, but I still said okay. I had no idea what to do in a relationship. I was a kid and nowhere near mature enough, plus my voice was still squeaky. Dinah said something stupid to me, something I am not repeating here because it was just silly. But it hurt my soul. As we know it isn't hard to do to a fourth grader; it's like poking your finger through a paper thin wall of confidence. Don't blame me, as a kid I didn't understand she was joking around with me.

After that happened I was avoiding Dinah left and right. This was totally immature, I admit. Eventually I had gotten enough of the avoiding and I confronted her. I made such a mistake. I said, loud as ever, surrounded by kids in the lunchroom, "I don't wanna be your boyfriend anymore." I didn't mean to say it in front of a whole bunch of students, I just didn't realize how many people were around us. Dinah turned red with embarrassment. Then she kicked me in the beans.

After all that I felt . . . well, nothing, honesty. I was as single as can be, on the floor holding my beans. Probably crying. Moral of the story: Don't be a 4th grader, I guess?

The next part of this story is the SLOW end of eighth grade. I don't remember why, but I fell mad hard for a girl. She was short and had glasses, and the most extravagant smile and voice. For an eighth grader, I was in love a little too much. We started the classic flirting back and forth until I eventually asked her out. She, of course, agreed. So we started dating and everything was cool. She would give me a little smile and hug me during first period almost every morning.

Then things near the end of the year got complicated. Of all the couples, we had to be one of the few who were going to separate schools for ninth grade and it messed up our relationship. Then one day we were walking home. I thought everything was cool, but then she broke the news that we should break up due to obvious reasons. When I heard those words come out of her mouth it was like my heart was ripped out of me. All new emotions came into play and I experienced the dark scary parts of my soul. It made me even more upset that it happened right before the summer; I knew I'd be thinking about the girl that broke my heart all during the best time of the year.

Ever since then I promised myself I'd never make the same mistake twice. I also became more realistic about not seeing too far into the future. Moral of the story: treat others the way you'd wanted to be treated, protect yourself before you get hurt, and don't start moving too fast, trying to rush the future.

Also, you don't have to take advice from me. I'm only a kid who got his heart broken, who eats junk food with a fast metabolism and plays video games with a good education. So, hey, you do you, boo boo.

STEPHEN GOMEZ

BEGINNING?

My mother likes to travel. Very early she told me and my brothers that she wanted us to learn more about the world around us. She told us that having materialistic things, just objects, wasn't worth more than traveling, learning, and experiencing new things. Therefore traveling out of the state and country has somewhat become a family tradition.

My mother was an immigrant. She moved from Trinidad with my family to America to live a better life. It was hard for her to adjust when she got here; she stayed in the house, not going anywhere because her mother (my grandma) didn't have enough money to go places. When she had me, and soon after, my brothers, she didn't want us to live the couch potato life she had endured most of her time in America. So when we got old enough to walk, we started traveling. I've been a lot of places, especially for someone my age.

For example, we traveled around New York State. We visited Niagara Falls, and that was crazy; before you even got to the water it was crazy. I never knew a waterfall could be like that. People had raincoats and umbrellas even though it was sunny out, and I understood why when we got closer. It was like it was raining, but it was just the spray off of the falls. There was a gift shop right before the waterfall, which made no sense to me because you got wet just going to the gift store!

We didn't know we would need a raincoat. I was like, oh my God, I need to go back to the hotel to change. My brothers were running around, they were so happy, I don't know how they didn't slip. There were so many people, not quite so many that you couldn't walk but enough to be like, wow, there are a lot of people. It seemed like there were people from around the world. There was a little diversity because everyone wants to see Niagara Falls.

We have travelled out of the country, too. For example, a few years ago we went on a cruise. When we first got on board we met lots of fellow passengers from everywhere. I was so surprised that people came from Germany just to take a cruise. I met other teenagers who came from England who said I had a New York accent. I had never heard that I had a New York accent.

Everyone was on the cruise. Caribbean kids. White kids. Russian kids. There was something called the o2 Club, which was for teens, broken down by age. Everyone thought I was eighteen but I was much younger.

One day everyone on the boat was dancing on the deck, not to the official "Electric Slide" song, but to something else almost like it. I don't know how people did that in their bare feet because the deck was so hot.

We had these moments that I will always remember, like when we were all dancing to Not-the-Electric-Slide and also just something simple: it was two o'clock in the morning and we were eating grilled cheese on the deck playing music and watching Big Hero Six. I had no curfew as long as I made it back to the stateroom alive. I couldn't go anywhere, right? That made it especially fun.

The cruise was a whole week, we visited Jamaica and St Lucia. Because the ship was so big, we had to take another boat sometimes to get the islands we would be visiting.

I tried some different things, like parasailing. When I was parasailing, I kept thinking man the water is so clear and then what if I fall and wow the water is so clear. I had a life vest on so I had a little reassurance. I will always remember that moment. I was experiencing an adrenaline rush and so much more at once.

When I floated back down, I was very glad to have my

feet on the boat.

I had seen a lot of graphic videos about jet ski crashes, so I didn't go jet skiing.

I did go on a canoe trip. We hit a rock near a whirlpool. We went under the rock and the boat flipped and everyone scattered, I was under the rock. That scarred me for life, I tell ya. Everything happened so fast. One second I was under the boat, then I got out and was okay.

They were all different experiences, good and bad.

Not bad like I don't want to travel, but bad like that's cool, but wow.

My mom says she doesn't want to spoil us with material goods, but she wants us to see things with our own eyes. She asks "how many of your friends go to the places you go to?"

When we travel, I feel rejuvenated from school especially when I have had a lot of homework and projects.

I understand the purpose of why my mom wants us to travel.

And I'm pretty sure I learned a couple things.

RAQUEL GRACIEN

BEHIND THE MASK

There were times where I cried,
Times where I wanted to die,
tears falling from my eyes

Dreading the nights where I felt like I was in a dark hole,
My mind wandering, and that's something I couldn't hold,
They told me don't worry,
it was gonna be okay
but was it really?

Praying for my downfall,
They were hoping I didn't make it,
Had to put on a fake act,
You gotta fake it till you make it

SAMOYA SALMON

BEING YOU?

Why should I change?
It doesn't hurt to be a little strange
We were told to be this and to be that
Why can't we just be this OR that
Does it hurt to be different?
Or to be indifferent
Why should people tell me who I should be
Shouldn't it be my choice to be what I should be

I was told that life brings a lot of possibilities
But I didn't know that it brings responsibilities
Through life, challenges comes along
It's not how we deal with them that makes us strong
But what we learn from them further on

BROOKE LYNN BASCOMBE

CONFESSIONS OF A BROKEN HEART

"Obstacles are put in your way to see if what you really want is worth fighting for."
        -Author Unknown

Every daughter needs a dad. Unfortunately, my dad broke my heart way before any boy had the chance to. Even though my mom left my dad, he was the one who made the decision to abandon me. He never visited me or called to check in to see how I was doing. He wasn't there for me at all. The older I got, the more abandoned I felt and the sadder I became.

On the other hand, my whole life my mom made sure that I got everything I wanted and needed without the help of my father, even though she couldn't provide the love of a father for a daughter. On my birthday and Christmas, my dad sent gifts; that's really the only time that I spoke to him. I remember one summer my dad took me to the mall and took me shopping for sneakers, since he knows that I love sneakers. I enjoy getting money and shoes from my father, but more than that, I wish my dad understood that I don't want or need the material things that he provides. The only thing I really want is a relationship with him.

Last year my dad came to New York for my aunt's baby shower; everyone was in one big room. There was music blasting, the smell of food, and people walking in and out. I saw him and my heart started beating very fast, like everything was moving in slow motion. I'm not sure what I expected. Maybe I thought we would have a detailed conversation about my life. Maybe I thought he would magically know all the right questions to ask. Unfortunately, we barely talked. I said hi, he said hi back. "How are you doing?" "Good." Then the conversation was over. The silence was awkward. We looked at each other for two minutes and then walked away. We talked like we were strangers, like I didn't know him at all. And he surely didn't know me. I had always felt that I was somehow not good enough for my father since he never visited me much. At the same time I was relieved knowing that it wasn't only me that he did this to. I know it sounds horrible, but it's the truth. I have other siblings and he isn't involved in their lives either.

I learned on social media--Facebook, to be exact--that I had siblings. It still hurts me when I remember finding out that way. Even though I don't have a relationship with my father, my siblings and I are determined to have a relationship with each other. I haven't met my siblings face-to-face yet, but one day we will have the opportunity to meet in person. Although we have not yet met, I keep in contact with them on the phone. When the day comes for us to meet, I don't want us to feel awkward talking; I want us to be comfortable. It's not my fault or their fault that we were never given the opportunity to know each other. I deserve a real relationship with them. I'm determined.

Despite the fact that I didn't grow up with my father I've had a fantastic life because I have the world's best mother. If she says she's going to do something she does it; no "ifs," "ands," or "buts." She's always there for me. I'm sure it wasn't easy, especially in the beginning, but my mom never disappoints me.

JOSEPHINE BIJOUX

CONFIDENTLY LOST

Breathe in, breathe out, breathe in, breathe out, breathe in, breathe out . . . why isn't it working!? God, what is wrong with me? You have to keep it together; you can't lose control. Not again, and definitely not now. I can't move. My body feels numb and I can't stop shaking! Do not cry, you have to be strong, you have to be perfect. But how? How can I be perfect? How can I keep it together right now? It's too much, I'm feeling too much. I'm angry, sad, and scared. God, I'm so scared. My heart is pounding so hard it feels like it's going to explode. The voices and sounds around me are starting to fade. I don't want to go back, I have to stay here, here is real and there is not. I feel like I'm fading away. Stay Calm. I can breathe. There's so much going on in my head, so many thoughts that I feel like i'm going to lose my mind. I'm getting dizzy and I'm starting to bring attention to myself. I wish Aubrey were here because she always knows what to do. I feel like I'm going crazy.

Just breathe.

Sometimes you need to remind yourself of who you are and who you want to be.

This is what anxiety feels like: the shortness of breath, feeling like you're about to have a heart attack, feeling overwhelmed by your emotions like you're losing control, and the feeling of intense fear that there's nothing you can do about it. I've been struggling with anxiety since I was eleven years old. My first attack was on January 12, 2010, the day I almost lost both my life and my parents.

I wanted so much to help people that day, but I couldn't. I was leaving to go to Florida in a week. I remember asking myself, "Why? Why me, God? What did you see that was so special in me? That you didn't see in them?" For months I wondered if I deserved it, did I deserve this second chance at life that God was giving me? For a long time I was angry with myself and at the world. I watched thousands of people suffering and dying and I did nothing about it. I was always the quiet and shy type of person, so I am very observant of my surroundings. But after this near-death experience I feel like God really opened up my eyes and my mind, and for the first time I was seeing the world very differently. I got to see how people can come together as a community and help each other, but I also saw how selfish people can really be and that bothered me.

Having an anxiety attack always trigger these awful memories. It feels like the earth is shaking again but this time I'm not in my house with my mother. These times I am always alone, surrounded by nothing but darkness, and it feels like the people I love and care about are being taken away from me.

* * *

"Jose, are you happy, like, truly happy?"

"Umm . . . Cindy, what are you talking about? I swear you ask the most random things. Can we just focus on this work? It's d--"

"Jose, I'm serious; just answer the question."

I met Cindy in the sixth grade. She was the type of girl who was always fun to be around, confident and smart. Plus she was a great friend, because I always felt like I could talk to her about anything and she wouldn't judge me or talk about me behind my back.

"Is anyone ever truly happy? I'm not sad, does that count for something? Or at least answer your question?"

After I was done answering Cindy's question, she studied me for a second then told me something that I would never forget: "Jose, I'm your closest friend. And from what you've told me so far about your life, it seems like you're hurting. Like you're still holding on to the past. It's okay to be angry and sad, but at some point you have to learn to let go of the past and forgive those who have hurt you. Just remember that forgiving doesn't mean forgetting."

Cindy's words made me smile. I had been so angry and frustrated that day, and she made me realize how lucky I was to be alive and to have a friend like her. In the end she was absolutely right. I was only having a bad day, not a bad life. I still had my parents and my sister. They will always have a special place in my heart, even though we are separated. I am in New York with my uncle, my parents live in Haiti, and my sister is in Boston. My parents always call me as much as they can and I'm connected to my sister through text messages and video calls.

> *Life becomes easier when you learn to accept an apology you never got.*
> *- Robert Brault*

Forgiving was one of the hardest things that I had to do, especially because I had to do it alone. In order to do it alone, I had to learn how to work on myself. I knew that I wanted a change; I was tired of always being angry and it was draining. I was so focused on proving everyone wrong. My own family members told me that I couldn't do "this" or "that" or that I wouldn't make it in life. It's funny because I always thought that those you called family were supposed to help and encourage you, not be the ones to hurt you the most. I had to let all that negativity go because I realized that I had to want it for myself. I had to work hard and succeed for me, not just to please everyone or to prove them wrong. I also wanted to work on me. I was tired of being shy and tired and of letting my anxiety get the best of me. I wanted to be confident, to go after the things that I wanted and not be scared of failing. I realized that one of the things that was triggering my anxiety was the holding everything in, not letting go of the past, not forgiving myself and everyone who has hurt me. Although I didn't think of these things every day, they were still in the back of my head, popping up at any moment in the day while I was doing my work or lying down at night. These memories would resurface out of nowhere and become overwhelming. Having to deal with all of this and school was just too much to take in at once. Having these memories at school became one of my main triggers that led to my anxiety attacks.One of my scariest anxiety attacks forced me to push myself for a change. It occurred in the middle of the night. I was sleeping, dreaming but I can't remember about what exactly. All I remember is that I woke up screaming. I couldn't breathe, so I rushed to the bathroom. I closed the door behind me and locked it, then held on to the bathroom sink trying to catch my breath. I remember staying awake all night, then going to school in the morning, putting on a front like everything was okay. This was by far one of the scariest anxiety attacks I'd ever had.

I never wanted to feel like that ever again so I continued to work on myself. I kept myself busy on schoolwork as much as I could. I stayed after school to get help on my homework, then I started to join extracurricular activities outside of school. I started to do things that I wouldn't normally do, like being a youth leader for my school community. These were all things that made me uncomfortable but I did them anyway, because I wanted to keep on improving and working through the things that scare me.

I practiced public speaking, even though it terrifies me. I also started writing poetry, which I find very therapeutic. I practiced my art skills and read many books because I love reading. All of these things help me let go of my anger. They became my coping mechanisms and helped me find peace with myself. All of this was hard but I did it.

Today I still struggle with anxiety and I still sometimes make mistakes. But through my struggles, I found that I had to get to know me in order to find myself. I found that I had to figure out how to be alone to be comfortable in my own skin. I have made mistakes in the past but I've learned from them; what I love most about myself is that I am constantly evolving. Although I still make mistakes and may feel lost at times, I am confidently lost.

> *It was when I stopped searching for home within others and lifted the foundations of home within myself I found there were no roots more intimate than those between a mind and body that have decided to be whole.*
>
> *- Rupi Kaur*

SHERELL HENRY

DEAR FUTURE CHILDREN

Dear future children,

The story of each individual is different. The way we live, the way we walk, how we talk, and what we dream. The tale of the child within the person is told differently each time. Each time the story is told it consists of the same events and people, but the feelings, thoughts, and emotional awareness are all grasping at the individual through the vivid memory. When we stop to look at the world around us, we guess how many aspects we have in common with people we don't know, those we call strangers. We don't see the challenges that each child grows with, a past of gruesome monsters lurking beneath their beds, the monsters who are tempted to leap from their closets to see the look of terror on their faces.

My mother's maiden name is Sherryann Vealva. When she married, her name then became Sherryann Wala. My father's name is Derrel Henry. My parents were both born in Trinidad but have lived in the U.S. for some years. When this story started I was eight years old and playing with my younger cousin Mya at my Aunt Babsie's house in Trinidad where I was living. It was late at night, and the moon and stars were shining bright and glistening. The moon shined silver and the sky was dark as if someone took a paintbrush, made it black, and then sprinkled white glitter above it. My cousin and I were chasing each other around the house. My heart was beating quickly. I ran as fast as I could, reaching my hands out in front of me to grab her. After I caught her, I stopped and walked slowly to let my heart rate decrease. The house phone rang. I answered and said politely, "Hello, good night." At that time the only thing that was running through my mind was going to get a cup of ice cold water. I was breathing hard and trembling from running around. The woman on the phone said, "Goodnight."

Instantly I knew who she was. With the high pitched voice and slight Trinidadian accent, it would have been hard to miss that it was my mom. I was really excited; I began smiling so hard that my teeth and cheeks started to hurt. The longer I spoke to her, the more nervous I got. Even my hands were sweating. She didn't call often.

"What are you doing? I miss you," she said. I was grinning from ear to ear as I pictured her standing in front of me, me running to her arms. I replied to her by saying "good" while dragging the sound of the letter O. We spoke on the phone for about two minutes before she popped a big question. "Do you want to come and spend a holiday with me, your brother, your sister, and your nephew?"

I was an eight-year-old who hadn't seen her mom in a while. I was so excited that I began to scream, "YES! YES! YES!" I began to jump up and down so high. I didn't even think that I might hurt myself on the couch that was right near me. She told me that I should start to get ready. She also told me I have a new nephew. I dropped the phone and ran out the hallway screaming, "I HAVE A NEPHEW!"

I grabbed Mya and held her by her shoulders, shaking her back and forth, telling her I was going to see my mom and that I'd just found out I have nephew. I told my cousin what my mom said, the cousin who I called Aunty Avion (she is about a decade and a half older than I am). About thirty minutes after I spoke to my mom, I started getting ready and soon it was time to leave.

After all of the excitement, my stomach was hurting. I started feeling nervous and then nauseous. I hopped in a car that was taking me to my grandparents house just a few minutes away from Aunty Babsie's house. I was more nervous than I'd ever been. I looked up to the sky and my eyes started to water, filling with tears that would not go back up.

I was feeling torn; I cried silently. I called my Aunty Babsie "Mommy" because I had been living with her in Trinidad. I wanted to cry to her and tell her how much I loved her and would miss her. They said I was only going to stay for a little while. Some part of it me knew it was going to be longer than that.

I reached my grandparents' house where I said my final goodbyes to my cousins, aunts, and uncles. We got into my dad's car and headed for the airport. The drive from Carital to Port of Spain in Trinidad was normally really long, but it felt faster than it should have on that night. On the way to the airport, I didn't say anything to my father. I guess I didn't know exactly what to say. My mind was exploding with questions about going on this trip. I was worried and doubtful about going. I was already missing my cousins and my granny before we even got the airport.

When we reached the airport, the car came to a stop and I looked out the window at the bright lights that mesmerized me and the many people in line waiting to check in. The more I thought about what was ahead of me, the more nervous I became. It was my first time flying by myself, and I was a minor so someone who worked with the airlines had to accompany me. I made it to the gate and then I just couldn't do it. I couldn't take the steps that would put me on a plane to enter an entirely different country, not even knowing what was waiting on the other side. I took three steps, then I ran back to give my dad a final hug. I made sure I held him tight. I did not want to let go. I kissed my little sisters and said goodbye to my stepmother. I took a deep breath and followed the young woman to the gate. I boarded the airplane with her and took a seat. I sat near a window, and as I looked out of it, I imagined everything that could possibly go wrong. I tried to look up and picture something better. I pictured myself in the place they called America.

I fell asleep, and the young woman who accompanied me came and tapped me on the shoulder and told me that we had landed at JFK Airport. She got my bag (which was filled with snacks) out of the overhead bin and held my hand. We walked through security and a really long hallway that had a lot of twist and turns. I thought it was really fun just walking through them. They reminded me of a worm wiggling around in the sand. This made me smile. As we walked we reached the end of the hallway and it opened into a large waiting area. There was my mother, waiting patiently! My mom took my hand and we talked together to the car; at that time she had a gray blue truck. We drove and we drove and we drove. My mom gave me her phone and told me to call my grandmother and tell her that I arrived safely. I entered my new home on Dumont Avenue in East Flatbush, Brooklyn. We lived on the fourth floor.

My visit of a few days turned into a week and a week turned into two. No one mentioned me going back to Trinidad. I was enrolled into a school not too far from where we lived. Moving from Trinidad to New York wasn't anything that I expected to happen. I didn't understand why I had been living with my Aunt in Trinidad and I also didn't understand why my mom was suddenly ready for me to live with her in Brooklyn. No one asked me what I wanted, so the only thing I knew to do was smile and move on. I started second grade and the journey to making new friends but I was a really shy kid. I didn't really speak to anyone and I stayed mostly to myself. I made a few friends early on who later turned out to be not real friends at all. When I started third grade was when I started to have my first real encounters with bullying. The "means girls" called me names and so did the boys. I was super sensitive and the names really hurt my feelings but I tried not to show it. I didn't want to show weakness and vulnerability in front of people who could potentially be my enemies.

I experienced bullying almost every day. If kids were not insulting me they were pushing and shoving me. One recess a boy took me by the sleeve of my sweater and swung me in a circle. I didn't make a big deal about it, maybe because I was shook, scared, and upset. I didn't like it but I didn't want to tell anyone. Instead I looked to what I could change about myself. I tried to find a reason why they disliked me. I thought they picked on me because I looked like an easy target, because I was shy and wouldn't fight back. But it all was hurting me inside. I don't think I was bullied because I was from Trinidad, but being bullied did make me want to go back to the time and the place I called my home.

One experience of bullying changed my circumstances drastically. During lunchtime in the auditorium I was goofing off and fell off the chair. The boy who, at the time, I considered my crush was sitting right in front of me and I asked if he could help pull me up. His way of helping was to pull my entire arm hard and make my forearm bang really hard right on top of the auditorium chair. In that moment all I felt was pain. I later realized that there was a swelling on my arm and it was really red. I showed my mom and told her what happened. That was the first time I ever told my mom about an incident where a bully hurt me. I never told her before but I felt that she needed to know this one. My mom was overprotective so she went up to the school and even called the police to file a complaint. Later that week I was removed from the school and since then I have never seen anyone from that school or any of those students who bullied me.

Being removed from that school put a form of relief in my heart but because of my experience with bullying I have put up a wall to protect me from people I feel I can't trust. I am very willing to let someone into my life, but I can just as easily remove that person. Coping with bullying was especially hard because I didn't speak to anyone about what I was going through, I mostly just kept my feelings bottled up inside.

I have learned to face the monsters under my bed and hiding in my closets. I can let them in by believing they exist and get rid of them by believing that they don't. I have also realized that not everyone is going to like you. Some people are going to despise you because to them you are a risk; you might have something they want or are maybe worried you might take something they have. Other times bullies are going through their own problems and need to pick on someone else to make themselves feel better. Now as a freshman in high school I am very mindful of those I call friends.

I have dealt with my monsters and I will continue to deal with them. For right now the best that I can do is leave the past in the past, use my experience to build my strength, and continue to be my strong, brave, smart, and beautiful self.

As a letter to my future kids I want you to know that I have sat and passed the most difficult, mind-breaking, and impossible tests, ones in which I was close to failing. You will always be tested so be ready to show your strong, brave, smart, and beautiful selves.

Sincerely,
Sherell.

ANNALISE THOMAS

FIRST DAY IN THE U.S.

At the age of six I was living a comfortable life with both parents and my brother in my wonderful home in Guyana. One day, my mother came to me and said, "We're going to America." I was shocked because I thought life was perfect where we were. I responded, "Huh?" She said, "Yes, you're going to get a better education, see new family members, make new friends, have an easier life, and see wonderful lights every night and beautiful fluffy snow." All of that seemed great to me. Honestly, I couldn't wait to move to America.

The night my mother told me this, I could barely sleep because I was so excited. The next day I went to school, super excited to tell my friends about the new place I'd be going to. I started describing the cold, icy snow and the magical lights that turned on every night. I also told them that I'd get to eat everything I wanted because America has all the world's best foods. They became as excited as I was!

The next few days went by fast. I was taken to the United States Embassy to get my passport, pictures, fingerprints, and visas. Later on I went to the doctor to get multiple immunizations and medical clearance. My mother and I were able to get our passports stamped which was proof that we were able to travel.

Finally it was time to take the flight to America. My mother and I made sure we had everything. I began to feel anxious and confused. I started to worry about what would happen next. How would I react to my new culture? Where am I going to live? Would I ever get to see my father again? How would my older brother feel knowing he was unable to come?

As we traveled to the airport, a lot of my family and friends came to say their final goodbyes. I felt as if I was leaving my entire life behind but still I was ready to see what all this hype over America was about. When we arrived at the airport my father and brother started crying. I assumed they were having the same thoughts as me. I said my goodbyes to everyone but I saved my father for the last goodbye. I wasn't uneasy about seeing my father crying because I completely understood why.

It was about seven or eight o'clock in the morning when we got on the plane. We handed in our tickets and looked for our seats. My mother put our bags up, sat down, and buckled our seatbelts. My mother decided to switch seats with me. She couldn't handle being on an airplane for the first time and looking out the window. When it was time to take off I felt like my stomach and head were leaving my body.

When we were officially in the air, I looked out the window and saw nothing but a tiny place that I thought was so big. When I looked to my left, I saw my mother acting as if her soul was leaving her body, she was so scared. Then she started to take really deep breaths which helped her feel better. I was looking out the window for the entire ride.

The flight attendants brought out our lunch; it was lasagna. When I took my first bite I was disappointed. It was squishy and not very well seasoned. Later, when we were close to landing, I started seeing so many different colored lights and huge buildings. I knew we were in New York.

When we landed we took our suitcases and exited the plane. As we were leaving the gate, my mother greeted a group of people that I'd never seen. To my surprise it was my grandfather and uncle, surrounded by other relatives who I didn't know. My grandfather handed huge jackets to both of us. I wasn't sure why he handed me the jacket, but I told him thank you. As soon as we walked outside I understood why. As we walked outside all the cold air hit me and I quickly dug my face into my jacket. On the way to my grandfather's house I saw zooming cars on the highways and ice on the windows and houses.

When we got to the house where we would live, we walked up the stairs that were covered in ice. My mom slid down the stairs on the ice. I guess it wasn't a good idea to wear heels on that travel day. We quickly put our bags down. We were leaving Brooklyn to go back to Queens to visit my grandmother. We went on the highway again with the zooming cars. When we arrived at the next apartment, I found two aunties and an uncle living there with my grandmother.

Unfortunately that was the moment my eyes saw something new. I saw my grandmother, lying on the living room couch, bald and dying from cancer. She was hooked up to a machine, with hardly any energy. It seemed like she was in a lot of physical and emotional pain. When it was time to leave we all got back into the car. My mother looked so sad now. When we got back to my grandfather's house I began unpacking. So much had taken place that I found it hard to sleep.

A few days later I started at my new school. It was certainly a lot different from back home. This school had security guards. I learned a lot about America in a few days! Some things were sad and some were a lot different from the country I left behind. Of course, my life is a lot different now from that of the six-year-old who came to America. I've learned a lot; I've learned to look forward to all the new things that are ahead of me.

HANNAH COOPER

GROWING WINGS

Whatever life throws your way, just be strong and fight through it. Just like when life gives you lemons, you make lemonade. Strong walls may shake but they never collapse. Growing up and living in a toxic home with constant arguments and fights affected me as a child. As a kid, I always wished to have a perfect life, a big happy family, nice Sunday dinners, and game nights. I daydreamed about growing up, having my big house, car, and husband, but really it's like I had the total opposite. Over the years, I've learned to stop dreaming and to face reality.

From the time I was a baby going into my teenage years, my parents would fight and argue all the time. I always felt like I wasn't good enough, like I had to be someone else for them to really love me. My mom and I never really had a mom and daughter relationship, and my dad and I were never really father and daughter. My mom would always try to keep my father out of my life for some reason, when he actually wanted to be a part of my life. I had so many questions and still until this day it triggers me. Sometimes I'd get beaten for even wanting to do better or be better and would cry myself to sleep. I'd cry in the shower sometimes so nobody would see me and ask questions. I was never really the type to express myself outwardly either, I would just bottle up my feelings and keep them to myself. That affected me in the long run. Any little argument I would get into, whether it was in school or at home, and all the built up feelings started to take a toll on me; I would just explode. My dean used to refer to me as a "firecracker" because one little thing and I'd just pop off. It made me laugh when she said that to me. I knew it was true.

Over time I felt as if my attitude and personality changed, like I gave up on family and friendships. I just had this "I don't care about anything" attitude. I also began to do this fake act, like a mask, trying to be something that I'm not to hide the hurt and pain. I would act like everything was ok when really, it wasn't.

"The hardest prison to escape is your mind" ~ Bob Marley

Sometimes we're our own enemy. We sabotage and overthink, and cause ourselves to be unhappy. We even stop ourselves from achieving greatness. Sometimes I would be my own enemy. I'd surround myself with the wrong crowd when all they did was hold me back from achieving my full potential. I began to slack in school and my grades went down the drain. My mother would get phone calls from my teachers saying how much potential I had, that they knew I was capable of doing the work. Everyone was expressing the belief that I didn't reach my full potential because I would care more about friends and impressing them rather than doing my school work. Depression had also hit me hard around that time, and that made me slack more with my school work.

I distanced myself from literally everyone. I'd be sad everyday, I didn't eat as much as I used to, and I didn't laugh or smile the way I used to; everything was different. The depression wore away at me for so long that I could no longer maintain that mask. Everyone saw through it, not only by my actions, but by my appearance. I'd look drowsy, my eyes were low, with bags under bags. I even lost weight over those months.

I didn't reach out to friends or people in my school. I always had my guard up and was pretty shy with meeting new people. I grew up not being able to distinguish healthy relationships with friends or family from unhealthy ones because I was like, in a dark hole because of not having my father in my life throughout my childhood. I didn't have a male figure to teach me the other aspects of life, like how should a boy treat me, or what to tolerate and what not to, those kinds of talks.

When I got older I was able to understand more and I contacted him independently. I later grew a bond with my father. He would take me out to eat and go shopping. He wanted me to stay in school and be successful. My father used to call me and tell me about my cousins, how they wanted me to come to family events and reunions and spend time with me. Two summers ago, I lost my grandmother, my father's mother. Although I didn't really know her it took a big toll on me. For years I'd heard, "Do you want to meet your grandmother? She's been dying to meet you and spend time with you. She wants to see what you're like." I think what triggered me the most was that I had to hear over the phone that my grandmother, who my mother denied me every opportunity to meet, had passed away. Not only was I hurt, but I was also angry. I tried several times to get closure, to understand why my mother makes the decisions she makes. Was I not good enough? Was I some kind of mistake? Did she have any regrets with me? She never had any answers for me. This affected even my school work. I missed out on several opportunities like college programs, tutoring, sports, and even trips. Anything extra related to school she didn't want it for me. She would tell me I wasn't capable of doing this and would doubt me. They say words don't hurt but her words stayed with me and scared me. Things like this made me feel unwanted and like my mother abandoned me. At times I didn't even want to be here; I didn't really see a point, and bottling up my feelings made it worse. Our family had problems, my sister struggled with her health, and my brother got locked up constantly for small, petty things.

There was a bit of a turning point in my life as the years went by, as I began to change my company, study more, participate more, and stay after school to get tutoring. I started to do well in school again. I started to set more goals and strived to accomplish them.

At the same time, my father and I got closer and closer. I'd call him for anything I needed, or even just to talk. Two years ago, my sister was blessed with the love of not only her life, but mine and gave birth to a beautiful baby boy. In school, more opportunities were open for me such as offers for college trips and Brooklyn College programs. I've been offered a spot in SAT prep and to join an AP class. I've made being involved in positive activities my highest priority and that has helped me overcome both my depression and the difficulty of my upbringing. It makes me feel like nothing is impossible to me.

NEIKA VICTOR

YOU MUST BE ON SOMETHING

You never see the wrong in your actions, you blame others for
   your lack of compassion
You've taken her youth, stolen her innocence without her
   permission
Unless it wasn't clear to you before she screamed NO!
Even as the words were trapped in her throat struggling to
   escape you proceeded
taking it as an invitation
Tell me, did you enjoy taking the life from her eyes?
ARE YOU SATISFIED?
The reflection of herself is a reminder of the memory that
   was latched onto her
Your cruelty has turned her cold, she's no longer bold
Now she blames herself and the way she expressed her
   personality through her clothes
It's funny really, how we shame females instead of teaching
   men that we are not sexual objects!
But society likes to teach us don't get raped, rather than
   DON'T RAPE!
 Because apparently her clothing being provocative meant
   she was asking for it
It's sick ! but in some ways I get it
Because some girls do use their outfits and body as permits
Like the way her skirt had that slit and the way she swayed
   her hips
Then hit the floor in a split
Like UH, that girl lit
But if you think that, that is an excuse for what you did then
YOU MUST BE ON SOMETHING!

GIVE ME YOUR EYES

Your eyes
Your eyes are the ones I seek
The way they shine so sleek
Your eyes are what I need
They take in everything, the way they feed
Your eyes I see so clear
They hold despair
All your deepest desires unacted and it's unfair

They see the world so differently
Finding beauty in everything and purpose in life
Oh how I envy your eyes and the way they glow in the night
Such a beautiful creature should not possess such dangerous
    weapons
Give me your eyes!
For mine are too blind to see
Give me the gift that no one else seeks

Tell me what you see when you look into my eyes?

When I look into your eyes I see a pair not so different from
    mine
I see the burden of every lost child
I see a lost soul trying to find light
Stranger with the dark eyes, I'll be your beacon but only if you
    learn to open your mind
I can't give you my eyes
For mine were born blind

I AM BLACK WOMEN

I am the sun
A star that wasn't made to fit in
A wildflower
Grown naturally
Untamed
I REFUSE TO BE CONTAINED!
I am poetry
A quality of beauty
And an intensity of emotions
My back carries the stories of my ancestors
That were silenced by whips
I am a woman of courage and strength
I am mother of life and temptation
My hair swirls and spins like the earth
My hips were born rolling with the tide
My skin is black diamond
My body is art
My heartbeat is the melody that puts babies to sleep
I am the woman that picks myself up every time I fall
I AM A FEMINIST!
I am cornrows
And everything that you see as ghetto!
I am a walking treasure
I am black and proud
You may not want me
But you want everything that I have!
From my lips to my hips
From my music to my slang
Who am I?
I am black women!
Our melanin is exquisitely beautiful
Our skin defines beauty YOU WILL RESPECT US!

TAKING CHANCES

My heart is not a tool
It's tired of being broken down and played with
Oh how you've let me down so many times but I stood by you
Just like a fool who was just too blind to see through you
Until the day that I realized
Your chains of lies were habits too light to be felt
You refuse to break your patterns because you are afraid that
 you'll finally feel
Feel the pain that you selfishly pushed aside!
My first thought was, how can a man be so cruel?
I took a chance and jumped with you
You shattered me into tiny little pieces
And I still picked them up while bleeding
And put them back into your hands
I TRUSTED YOU! And for a while we were happy
But you still couldn't see that
Your mind does not have to be your prison
You don't have to stay locked up in the past that has let you
 down so many times!
I saw the love in an empty heart and selflessly made it mine
 Why do you put yourself through this?
Why do you stay with him?
To answer your questions
I had a lot of reasons to give up on him, but choose to stay
 because he's been hurt by people who
Have never been taught how to love. He once took my pain
 and made it his own, he saved me! So why shouldn't I save
 him?

You tell me that my opinion makes me less beautiful
Try silencing me again and this tongue will cut you

I AM BEAUTIFUL BECAUSE I HAVE OPINIONS

You grow up believing in fairytales
Then the world rips the innocence from under you
They tell you that fairytales are for children
So you grow up into someone who can't see the magic that
   surrounds you

HUMAN NATURE

IVANCILE JULES

MY LAST PLAYOFF GAME OF THE SEASON

It was a dim afternoon. We had just finished a long, vigorous week of football practice and it was now winding down to the last few minutes of it. Coach C. finally called us over with a whistle and said, "Beep, beep, beep. Okay guys, bring it in. Take a knee and quiet down. Tomorrow, as you all know, is a playoff game, meaning if we lose tomorrow this will be the last practice of the season. And the last time most of you seniors will ever play football again." As he said this, I looked around at the other players. I wanted to see what their facial expressions were in response to the coach's speech wondering if they were still as excited as I was, even though this could potentially be the last game of their miniature careers. For the most part I was still excited and enthusiastic, probably because I was still a junior at the time. I knew I would be able to play football next year, God willing, as long as I didn't get hurt in the off-season.

As I continued to look around, I saw some faces that were sorrowful and some that were doubtful. Maybe they thought we couldn't win. But I still saw some fierce and enthusiastic attitudes in most of the players around me. The coach finished his speech off with this: "Fellas, I want you to look to your left and right and understand that when you step on the field tomorrow, the ones you're looking at now will be the ones you're fighting for during our next game. I assure you, if you vow to give this game all you've got, there is absolutely no doubt in my mind that we can go out and win this game! We can prove the city wrong, prove people wrong, and move one step closer to a City Championship Title! Bart, breakdown the practice."

The players all cheered. Our team captain, Bart, yelled, "BREAK ON ME, BREAK ON ME. Championship on 3. 1--2--3!" The players roared, "Championship!!"

"The field house will be open at 8:15," Coach C. yelled over the commotion of the eager players. And we all went home.

The next day when I woke up, I immediately looked at the clock and it read 6:30 A.M. I thought to myself, "Thank God." This would be the worst day for me to be late; Coach would have killed me. I swiftly got out of bed, turned on my music, and played the Ray Lewis motivational speeches that I like. This is my ritual that I did every week before a game. Honestly, it helped me clear away any jitters so I could become mentally prepared for the game. I'm sure many players have similar ways of preparing themselves for a game. It seems pretty common. I proceeded to head for the shower, then got dressed and put on my clothes. I texted the varsity group chat in hopes to get a reply, given that it was still early in the morning. I texted confidently, "RISE AND SHINE, IT'S BEAST MODE TIME. LET'S GET THIS, FELLAS." I was proud to see that I got a lot of responses: flexing arms, thumbs up, and emojis. I was quick to walk out the door at what had to be about 7:00.

I unlocked the first lock on my front door and my father yelled with urgency in his voice, "Ivan, did you take your vitamins? Did you even eat breakfast?" I replied no and he gave me a few dollars so I could go to the local deli and order a warm breakfast sandwich. I thanked him and continued to unlock the door.

Every morning I ran through an obstacle course that is called an early morning public transportation commute in Canarsie. On the weekends it was an especially daunting task because the buses take forever to come.

When I finally arrived (on time, mind you) I saw that the same man who stressed most about being on time to morning meet ups was late: Coach C. himself, oddly enough. He arrived ten minutes past start time with a sorry excuse. "Sorry fellas, I was running trying to get you guys some bagels for breakfast." We didn't reply with much, just a simple "Good morning, Coach," with rushed smiles that implied we were thankful but just wanted to get into the field house, where it wasn't warm but still wasn't as cold as outside. Coach C. allowed us to blast hype music on the loud speakers but only on game day. I didn't usually get to play any of my music because the other players don't seem too fond of it. It didn't bother me much. I didn't really like their music either so I just wore my headphones.

Late stragglers started to slowly roam into the field house. Other players went out to grab breakfast; this time of day was usually the calmest. Shortly after that, when we were just about too comfortable, Coach C. blurted once again, "Fellas, start getting your equipment ready. The bus will be here soon."

Now take a moment to imagine what it's like to be in a room the size of an average basement with thirty-five plus people all changing into their football equipment that they've been wearing all week long. It didn't help that my locker was next to one of the sloppiest lineman you'll ever meet. I bet I'm the only one that would have put up with his bad habits without giving him too much of an earful.

"THE CHEESE BUS IS HERE!" yelled the players who were hanging outside the field house. Players and coaches started hustling their way onto the bus, with their expensive headphones and dazzling colors. That moment, with everyone getting on the bus, the excitement: you know it's really game time. The thing that's different about going into a playoff game, though, is that the tension is even more tense. Again, if we lose this game, there ain't no next week game.

Everyone finally boarded the bus and I sat next to my best friend Cameron, which is what I usually did. Cameron and I go to the same school on our campus (our school is in a large building that has been broken up into many schools) and we both have a common interest in football so he's kind of by default my best friend.

Coach C. requested that we travel in silence, presumably because he thought it would enhance our focus before the game. What felt like four hours was actually two, on a cramped school bus traveling all the way to Staten Island. We finally arrived and I was pleased to stretch my legs for a short amount time and get off the dingy school bus. We had to hustle to get in two lines and carried all our things onto the field for pre-game warm-up. Pre-game warm-up was helpful for those players who were nervous or who liked to warm up their muscles and go over the game plan. I usually took this time to see the trainer so that she could wrap my ankle with her special tape for extra support. This was because the position that I played, linebacker, was very demanding and required quick explosive bursts of energy and physicality. So it didn't hurt to take precautionary measures. About five minutes before kickoff (start of the game), Coach C. called the players who were game captains: Bart, G-rod, and Abu. They went over to the middle of the field to meet the referees for the coin toss. Meanwhile, other players gathered themselves, locked arms, and waited for the results. Unfortunately, we didn't win the toss and the other team decided to take the ball to start the first half. I didn't find much wrong with that because I personally liked getting to the ball to start the second half. It's a strategic advantage and helps if you're behind at the half.

The game started and players ran out onto the field for kickoff. One off the players yelled over the noise of the crowd, "Aye yo, Vikings, are ya ready?!" and we replied with much intensity, "Hell yeah!" The kicker kicked the ball. We stopped them around the twenty-eight yard line. Apparently Curtis, the school we were playing against, planned to run the ball to begin the game. They were successful enough to have scored the first drive of the game, which is something we have gone through with other teams, but we just had to find a way to minimize their scoring ability. With the first score being 7-0 with Curtis leading, we got ready for the kick return. Our offense had a tough time with their defense; in fact, we couldn't score any points until our fourth offensive drive. By that time the score was 14-0 in the first quarter. I had about five key tackles.

After our first touchdown, players started to feel hopeful again, like we were still in the game. With the score being 14-7 we started saying things like, "Yeah, they won't know what hit them after today. We're the underdogs," and "We ain't come out here to take no L." The confidence was contagious. We had reason to feel proud of how we played. After all, this was one of the top three teams in the city. Curtis was the championship title winner the previous year. They even beat us during the regular season 34-0. People expected us to get blown out by the first half, but we were hanging in there with one of the best. We insisted on staying focused as a unit because we didn't want our history with this team to repeat itself.

We started to gain momentum on defense; we were stopping their offensive run game and I even got a quarterback sack. All was okay for the first half of the game. Their quarterback was even getting frustrated with his offensive line, telling them, "Oh my God, can you guys just block?!" Things started to go in our favor toward the end of the first half, but the second half things started to change.

We successfully scored once more to begin the third quarter, with the score being 14-14, but the Curtis quarterback lobbed the ball up to one of his receivers who caught it over our smaller defensive back. Curtis scored seven more points.

Our team had one distinct weakness as a defensive unit: we had a hard time protecting the touchdown area from teams that can throw the football successfully down field. Curtis quickly exploited that. The score was now 21-14, then shortly after that they scored again. They had a lead of 28-14.

On the sideline players were getting upset that our offense couldn't score and that our defensive backs couldn't guard their match ups. I was slightly disappointed as well, but I am keeping hope during hard times. Attitudes and energy changed, and it seemed like we were accepting our soon to be fate of losing in the second round of the playoffs. I personally disliked when the team got like this. It disgusted me. Why was some players' drive to win gone after all we fought for during the regular season? As the game clock continued to wind down, the final score was 35-14 and the game was over. Curtis High school went on to the third round in the playoffs and eventually won the champion title again later that year.

If there is one thing I learned from this game, it's that it takes chemistry, drive, and patience to win a championship. But that's not enough: if you give up in the face of adversity you shouldn't even discuss the word champion. Championship takes full commitment.

JUST LET IT FLY

Just let it fly.
I'm the kind of kid that'll never let my dream die,
With me they will always stay alive.
In this life I'll always strive,
But just to keep in mind
The risks you take may result in a steep dive.
Still never let it deter you from the try.

Just let it fly.
My life I own up to because it's mine.
The difference between me and you
Is a bright red line;
I must warn you, if you cross it,
What you see may not be too kind.
But if you invite me to your side of the line,
Enlightenment is what you'll find.
My smile would lighten your day like sunshine,
You wonder if this must be a sign,
So just let it fly.

TELENA SMITH

AS TOLD TO AR'MAUNIE BLALOCK

OVERCOMING

When we are young we have many dreams. Some of us wish to have a family or dream of running a huge company like Microsoft or being a reality TV star. Depending on the environment we are exposed to, our choices can change and our dreams can diminish.

Telena Smith began swimming when she was two years old, and began swimming competitively when she was six years old. At nine, Telena felt that she had the world to conquer and was determined to swim in the 2012 Summer Olympics. Four days a week she began at five in the morning; her mom and dad took turns waking her up and making sure she arrived at Castellani Swimming Pool to train for the day. Telena traveled four days a week and on those chilly, dark mornings, she loved to breathe in the crisp fresh air even though the forty-five minute car rides were quite bumpy. For these childhood years Telena's entire world revolved around swimming. But the Olympic dreams of that little swimming girl were erased on April 8, 2009, when she left her home country of Guyana to come to New York.

Compared to her home country of Guyana, her small corner of New York wasn't that big, but it still frightened her. This fear was deepened because she made the journey without her best friend, her mother. She was in a strange place facing every fear without her mom by her side. Telena missed her mother so much it was like she was a puzzle that was incomplete, because her mother was the main piece. Her mother had brought out the best in her. Even at this young age Telena understood that she wasn't the only one making a sacrifice. Her father sacrificed, too, leaving her mom and the rest of his entire family to bring his daughter to America. Her mother sacrificed years of not living with her husband and only child to ensure that her daughter could obtain an education.

Telena's childhood in Brooklyn was so different from her childhood in Guyana. No more days spent swimming or talking for hours with her mom. There were no more early wake up calls. She missed the joy of sacrificing to do what she loved. Instead, Telena's day began at 7:30 a.m. No longer was she the passenger in the family car on the way to school. In America her father left early to go to work. Most days, Telena walked to school.   Alone.   The quiet was overwhelming, especially when she observed other kids her age accompanied on their path to school by siblings and parents. During her short walk from home to school, she concentrated on the bright sun, the trees sprouting beside the sidewalk, and any little bit of nature. She focused on anything but her mother, because when her thoughts drifted to her, she remembered one thing and one thing only: just how much she missed her mom. Her focus turned from swimming lessons and private school to sitting in a large classroom at P.S. 203. School itself was so different than in Guyana; no green and white uniforms like she wore back home. More shocking was the disrespect she felt her American classmates showed their teachers. Talking back to teachers? That surely would not have been tolerated back home. Telena recalls how her face dropped the first time a classmate talked back to a teacher and nothing happened to the student.In order to rise above her despair, Telena focused on school, even in the fourth grade. Telena figured if her parents sacrificed everything for her to come to New York for a better education, then Telena would make sure that their sacrifice was worth it. Telena also surrounded herself with good friends who became her extended family. As she grew up, she let the hard hours of loneliness fuel her compassion for helping others.

Telena is now a student at Daemon College in Buffalo, New York and earned a spot on the Dean's List her very first semester. Even through the tough times, like leaving her home country and many of her loved ones behind, she summoned her inner strength, found support, and was able to still find herself.

AUBREY BIJOUX

AS TOLD TO JOSEPHINE BIJOUX

SHE WHO DARED LEAD HER OWN PATH

Since you all got to read my story, here is the story of someone who holds a very special place in my heart. She is my best friend, my teacher, my biggest supporter, and one of my role models: my older sister.

"Some women fear the fire. Some women simply become it."

-R.H. Sin

My sister Aubrey moved to New York from our home in Haiti when she was only twelve years old. Sending her to the U.S. was probably one of the hardest decisions that our family had to make. It was necessary because back home wasn't safe during this time; children were being kidnapped and raped, crime was very high, and people were sometimes randomly killed. It especially wasn't safe if you went to a certain kind of school and looked a certain kind of way. By this I mean that you were in danger if you were thought of as pretty, had a nice skin complexion (or really, met any of their physical requirements), or if your parents were fortunate enough to get you into a very good school. Good schools are expensive in Haiti and when you are seen going to a such a school you can become a target. Our parents were fortunate enough to build this foundation for us where we had everything a child in our country could ever want: a nice home, access to the best education, beautiful clothes, and lots of supportive friends and neighbors. But because this form of targeted crime got so bad, my parents began to ask themselves if a great education in an unsafe place was worth it. They worried they were putting their eldest daughter's life in danger. So my parents decided to send my sister to New York to live with our uncle, that is, our father's brother.

Aubrey had to adjust to a new life where everything was different from what she was used to. The city was bigger than what she was used to, and it was cold. There were so many lights and everywhere you went you could smell fast food in the air. Add to that she was around a new family that she wasn't very familiar with. Adjusting to her new life was challenging but luckily she had our grandmother there visiting during this time. Our grandmother being in New York gave my sister a sense of warmth, a reminder of home and everything that she loved about her life in Haiti.

"People say things meant to rip you in half, but you hold the power to not turn their words into a knife and cut yourself."
-Rupi Kaur

A couple of years later, just as Aubrey had begun to adjust to her new home, she received some very big news. She was told she needed to move to Florida to live with another uncle, this time my mother's brother. She needed to move because our uncle in Florida had legally adopted my sister when she was eight (although she didn't live with him or know him very well) and now he was finishing the paperwork for her so that she could receive her green card.

This was a sad change for my sister because she just started to adjust to her new home! Now she had to move to another place that was once again foreign to her. Keep in mind that she knew this uncle (our mother's brother) just as much as she knew the first uncle she went to live with (our father's brother), meaning not very much at all. Both uncles only came to Haiti every now and then, and sent back school supplies, shoes, and backpacks when family members would visit. Sometimes they sent money on holidays, birthdays, just because, or if there is a family emergency.

So this was her new beginning, she went from bright

city lights, corner stores, and fast food restaurants everywhere to a suburban setting in Florida. But surprisingly she found that adjusting there was easier. Uncle's wife Rachel made her feel welcome and so she felt more at home. She was happy that she didn't have to follow so many strict rules this time; she just had to go to school and to church and she even had her own room with her own TV!

Aubrey graduated high school in 2012, but she couldn't go to college because she still didn't have her green card. She came from Haiti under Temporary Protected Status (TPS) which allowed her employment authorization. She started working at Toys "R" Us and had a babysitting job with a church friend. But as a TPS card holder in Florida, you are charged out-of-state tuition. Also, TPS doesn't allow you to receive any government grants or loans to go to college. Minimum wage and a babysitting job were not going to cut it. Aubrey finally got her green card the second summer after she graduated high school. She thought she was headed to college, but for no reason that I can understand our uncle didn't want to give her his tax information and she couldn't file an application for financial aid. This news was devastating to her; she was sad and angry. Instead of taking her anger out on the world, she continued working at Toys "R" Us, babysitting, and going to church. As time passed, Aubrey knew she wanted more for herself. One night she called one of our cousins who lives in Massachusetts and he told her about this program called Year Up. Year Up is a one year career development program that includes college-level courses and a six-month professional internship in information technology or financial operations. Year Up in Massachusetts has a partnership with Cambridge College so you can earn 24 college credits, and there are Year Up programs across the US that have partnerships with nearby colleges. Aubrey was very excited to learn about the program, but when she looked it up the closest Year Up program near her was three hours away from home in Miami. This was too far for her to attend since the program doesn't provide housing. She was disappointed until she gave our cousin another call. He had a great solution: she should move to Massachusetts to live with him and his older sister! Wanting to seize control of her life, my sister made a call to our parents and told them of this great opportunity. Our parents were supportive of her decision. Then she made the best decision for herself: she packed her bags and moved to Massachusetts and while living there she motivated our older cousin to join the program. She is working now.

I am so proud of my sister and the woman she has become. Aubrey is one of the strongest people that I've ever met in my life. She's had so many challenges thrown her way and instead of backing down she stepped up and took control of her own path. She's not just my sister, she's my best friend. She is the only person that has always stuck by my side through my ups and downs; she always motivates me to be the best version of me. This is her story.

"Do not go where the path may lead, go instead where there is no path and leave a trail."
Ralph Waldo Emerson

AR'MAUNIE BLALOCK

SURPRISES

Life can be full of surprises; some are more heartbreaking and life-changing than others. And sometimes happiness can be an illusion. You think that everything is alright when it really isn't.

That's how I felt when I found out my dad had a rare bone cancer called multiple myeloma. He looked so healthy, but he went into the hospital and was there for over a week. When my mom finally told me about his diagnosis, I felt so anxious; I was worried we wouldn't have him with us very long. The longer he was in the hospital the more worried I got.

We visited him in the hospital and because of the treatment he had a weakened immune system. We had to wear masks and keep washing our hands, all the time! That was annoying and also scary. He seemed so tired but I could tell he liked having us visit. His room had a big picture window looking over the lights of Manhattan and it was amazing to see at night. It was weird to look out at the pretty lights, such a beautiful scene, from my dad's lonely scary hospital room.

My heart really hurt when we went to the hospital to spend Thanksgiving with my dad. I felt sad for him to be in such a place for the sick and ill, where happiness isn't normally found. Though my dad seemed happy to see his wife, children, and brother around him, I knew in his heart he would have been much happier in the comfort of his own home. I would worry for my dad. I knew was getting stronger, but it didn't decrease the long nights without sleep.

Plus, home didn't feel the same without my dad. It seemed . . . quiet. The living room TV rarely came on, and everyone seemed to stick to themselves. My little sister, who was the sun of the house, seemed to be cast out by clouds.

One day, when my dad still wasn't home, my mom came into my room with her nose in her phone and earbuds in her ear. It looked like she might be on the phone, with whom I didn't know. She can be such a phone junkie. My sketchpad sat on my lap, and I tapped my pencil against the paper, anxiously. Her face switched between several expressions: happy, to confused, to disgusted. Looking back I think she may have been disgusted or confused because my dad was explaining the many preparations the house would need for his arrival since the treatment had weakened his immune system. I puckered my lips and scanned my room that I shared with my little sister. "So--""Shush, Maunie, don't interrupt!" she said, putting her pointer finger up, with a scowl, to her face. I stared deadpan that she cut me off like that.

"Okay, then . . ." I thought, going back to my sketching. She sat at the foot of my bed causing the comforter to dip due to the extra weight. Finally, after what seemed like hours with her on that phone call, she finally hung up. A grin brightened her beautiful, yet sometimes scary features. This sudden grin made me feel very awkward. "And you're smiling like that why?" I asked, scooching back.

She began giggling like a schoolgirl, she was so excited. "You're gonna be very happy to hear this!"

"I am?" I said, though I didn't sound too enthusiastic because I was being my usual stoic self. My mind was racing for any surprise or ideas of special news she might want to share with me. Her grin turned into a sarcastic smirk, and she said, "No." I returned that smirk. I could be sarcastic just as well as my mom. That has gotten me in trouble a few times with her. She dismissed me and was about to get up. I sighed in defeat. "No! Please tell me! I'm dying to know!"

She chuckled and said, "Well, I just got off the phone with your dad, and--" I practically jumped on her, excitement bursting in me. Her eyes widened. "Okay... He was talking to his doctor. The doctor did have some good news to share, and it's that your dad is being released from the hospital, which also means he'll be home for Christmas."

I was excited about my dad coming home, but I was not as excited about decorating for Christmas. My cousin Yeshi had come over to help. I would moan and groan and complain about having to go downstairs and upstairs in a rapid, repeated sequence. "You need to stop bein' lazy," Yeshi said.

"Yeshi, hush. I don't need your big mouth yappin' at me; I'm really tired," I said, collapsing on my couch in the living room. I walked from the Christians tree, across the bar, and under the TV. My little sister Brooke tried to help, but she would often drop ornaments which would cause my mom to shake her head.

"No! Gimme!! I want it!!" Brooke began stomping her little feet.

"Brooke, stop it! You're gonna break them!" my mom said with annoyance. Brooke crossed her little arms and stormed away. I heard her mutter, "I don't like you." Yeshi must've heard it, too, for it made us laugh as we sat on the couch. Brooke's mouth spun up from a pout to a grin.

"I can't stand her little butt!" my mom said in a joking manner, hanging the ornament up. My Aunt Salema came to pick Yeshi up a little while later. So it was just my mom, my little sister and brother, and me at home.

The next day our family was back to its full size! My mom went to pick up my dad at the hospital. Joy swelled inside of me as I saw him and I greeted him with a huge hug as he wrapped his huge arms affectionately around me and my siblings. The house felt as though it was back to normal. Well . . . a little bit. My dad was a tiny bit grumpy, but he looked exactly the same physically except that he was bald and had lost his beard as well. He did still have his eyebrows! I loved having my dad back, I really did, and I'm sure that everyone else in the house did, too. Christmas was literally two days away and I'd never been so excited. My mom even had a party planned for my dad.

When it was finally Christmas day, I woke up early, just like every Christmas.

My mom was always nagging at me, on how I didn't wake up like this for school, I would respond, "Well duh, Mother, it's called excitement!" That would just make her roll her eyes. I tried to go back to sleep because it was eight in the morning. I wanted to get up and literally kick everyone out of their beds. After an hour went by I eventually heard the floorboards creak outside the bedroom, which meant either my mom or dad was awake and going into the living room. I immediately jumped out of bed! It was my mom in the kitchen. I heard the sound of more weight on the floor and turned to see my dad.

"Merry Christmas!!!" I said cheerfully.

My mom smiled and replied, "Merry Christmas, 'Mauna."

My dad flicked the TV on as he plopped on the couch. I heard feet scampering up the stairs and my little brother's beady head appeared through the doorway. "Merry Christmas, Edwin," mom said to him. He replied semi-groggily, rubbing his eyes.

"We have to wait until Brooke wakes up," my dad said.

My brother and I gawked in annoyance. "What?! Why?!" I said.

"Yeah, Brooke never wakes up," said Edwin.

"Doesn't matter, she can wake up on her own," my dad retorted. I sighed and plopped on the chair. Impatient, I decided to wake her up myself. My parents didn't see me disappear to the back where Brooke was sleeping, but a few minutes later they heard what sounded like a elephant running down the hall.

"Morning, Brooke, Merry Christmas," my mom said cheerfully, picking her up. Brooke smiled slightly, rubbing her eyes and yawning. My brother and I wasted no time to rush under the tree and tear open the gifts. My mom had gone into the kitchen, then reappeared with a pink jelly-like substance.

"What is that?" I asked as she put it in front of my dad. "Custard."

I sat down on the floor, next to the coffee table, with a spoon my mom had given me. I took a small scoop. It was a tiny bit sweet, but it was thick and beyond that really had no taste to it. I scrunched up my face in slight disgust. "It tastes weird" Edwin muttered.

As I watched Brooke and Edwin finish tearing open their gifts, I smiled. Then my oldest sister, Nena, also made a special star appearance when she knocked on the door. She didn't stay too long, just enough time to give our dad and me our gifts then she was on her way again back to the Bronx. Seeing her leave left some weight on my heart, because I didn't get to see her very often. But it was a nice surprise for her coming, even if she only stayed for a few hours. She had left me a book, a new title I had never even heard about.

It was good to have just the immediate family for the first few hours. It wasn't until later that extended family and friends start arriving. I'm not a fan of big crowds, so I went downstairs with Edwin and Yeshi. We stayed down there doing reckless things like playing a game we made up called "knock-over" using computers chairs. All you had to do was try to knock the other person off their chair with yours. We made a bit of a mess, though, and didn't bother to clean it up. Some hours passed and people started to leave.

My mom had invited people over for Christmas without telling them it was a homecoming for my dad; he didn't want people to come around just because he was sick. Spending that time with family and friends without talking about cancer was good for my parents; I could tell by the smiles on their faces. A year later my dad did announce his sickness, when his life was no longer in danger. My dad is better now, much better. At first he wasn't allowed to even go out of the house, but now he travels anywhere he pleases. I'm happy for my dad, and proud that he didn't let his sickness get to him, and proud to tell people my dad is a cancer survivor.

AMALAA JOSEPH

THIRTEEN HOURS APART

You all may know me as a fun, outgoing, bubbly tenth grader. But what you didn't know is I went to China. Yes, China. Across the world China, different time zone China, miles away China. I can honestly say it was the experience of a lifetime. It changed me for the better and a little for the worse. It was physically and mentally draining. I went without my Mom in a group of people. It was April of my sixth grade year, and I was eleven years old.

When the time for the trip came, I was ready for an adventure into a very different environment and time zone. There would be thirteen hours separating me from my mom. This would be the furthest I've ever been from home and her. I was excited but also nervous. It felt like I was leaving my mother for weeks. I remember going to the airport, meeting up with my group. I was the youngest one on the trip and it was a little intimidating, but there were girls there who took me under their wing and made me feel safe and happy. That made me think, Oh maybe I can get through this trip. When times for goodbyes came, I knew it would be the last time I see my mom face-to-face for a few days. I remember her looking at me, smiling so big. "You're growing up," she said. I felt so happy seeing her smile at me. When it was time to go I yelled out, "I LOVE YOU MOMMY," and she replied saying, "I love you, too, have a great time."

Soon I found myself sitting on a plane, feet in the air. The view was amazing. The beautiful white clouds and light blue sky made me stare out the window. I fell asleep for a few hours and then woke up, watched some television, and saw that "oh no, there are six hours still left." I fell asleep again and woke up for dinner. Finally, thirteen hours later, I arrived in Beijing, China. By then it was nighttime and I was exhausted. I just wanted to sleep my life away. We got to the hotel and I was sharing a room with two girls who were both in seventh grade. I got along with both of them and I was excited to be roomed with them. I thought we'd have fun.

Boy was I wrong.

I couldn't wait to call my mom. But unfortunately, she would have to call me in order for me to talk to her, which she did. The night I arrived I was happy and I was happy the next day as well. We got to experience (and climb!) one of the world's most famous monuments, the Great Wall Of China. We also visited the Temple Of Heaven and Tiananmen Square. Beijing was amazing.

But then the trip got harder because I started having roommate problems. I was going to take a shower, but turned around when I remembered that earlier that day my roommate said something mean about me. I confronted her and she got so defensive, like it was my fault. That was my first bad roommate experience.

Because my mom wasn't there, at first I thought there was no one to talk to talk to, but there was: a parent who came with her daughter, Ms. Jones. She helped me and was there for me when I was upset. I left my room to talk to her, and she said, "Don't worry, all will get better." I thanked her and went back to my room much calmer.

The next day we left Beijing for Shanghai. I knew I was gonna have to have another roommate, and that made me nervous because the girl who was going to be my roommate had been friend of mine. Until right out of the blue, before we moved into the room together, she was giving me the cold shoulder, ignoring me, being mean. I didn't know why. So when I found out we were going to be roommates I wasn't sure how it would go. My mom called just as we got in our room. I told her, "I don't think my roommate likes me." She replied, "Why do you think that?" I said, "She's ignoring me and we were cool before."

I guess my roommate heard my phone conversation and decided to comment, saying, "You're just really loud and annoying." I said I was sorry and we hugged it out and were cool again. I was happy. It put my mind at ease and my mom was happy as well. Besides all that roommate drama, Shanghai was beautiful. We got to go inside one of the world's tallest buildings: Shanghai World Financial Center. We got to the top floor, which was the 101st floor. It was like flying off the ground in a airplane when going up in the elevator. My ears popped and I needed gum. When we got up to the top, we were so high up it was crazy. I looked down and everyone and everything looked like ants. It was really foggy, being we were very high up and it was a cloudy day because it was gonna rain. It was amazing.

It was time to leave and eat. China and New York are very different when it comes to food. The food in China is different from the food in New York. It's not like your Brooklyn fried chicken and french fries. There were vegetables mixed with different things, rice with every meal you eat, which I love. After eating, it was time to go back to the room.

We weren't supposed to leave our rooms for other people's rooms, but with the day I had, I needed to go be with other kids. As I was leaving, I told my roommate, "I'm taking the key." She said, "No, leave it. Just knock, I'll be up." She was already lying down looking comfortable and about to fall asleep, but I took her word for it and said ok. I went into my friends' room and sat with them for a few.

All of a sudden the phone rang and it was Ms. Jackman, who was head of the whole trip for us. I guess she heard my voice and said, "Amalaa, you better be in your room by the time I get up there." Her voice gave me so much fear that I immediately left and went to my room. I banged and screamed for my roommate and she wouldn't answer. I was so mad and scared, I went back to my friends' room and sat there. Ms. Jackman came and she was furious. She walked me to my room and asked me questions like Where is your key. Why did you leave the room when I told you not to. As she asked that I started bawling really big tears. I explained that my roommate was horrible to me and explained the key situation. My heart was beating too fast and I was breathing so hard. All I could think about was my mom, sleeping, and going home. We called the front desk for them to open the door. As I was waiting it was an awkward silence. I was shaking, crying, everything was numb. When I got inside, Ms. Jackman tried waking my roommate but she wouldn't wake up. I felt she didn't believe a thing I said, that she didn't care about how I was feeling. I needed to hear my mom's voice. I texted her to call me and she did with no hesitation. I answered breathing hard and crying my heart out and I could barely speak. My mom asked what was wrong and I told her and she didn't know what to do or say in the moment. I noticed my suitcase lock was missing and I told my mom, "My lock's missing. I think my roommate took it but I don't know." I then started yelling to wake her up. My mom wanted me to put her on speaker. My mom doesn't have much of a filter, so she told my roommate, "Watch how you speak to my child; this whole thing is ridiculous." I had to get water and calm down because I felt my blood pressure rising and my heart beating.

My mother almost went to hospital. All this stress of me and her not being able to do anything because we were so far, and hearing me cry, was a lot for her. Her blood pressure got higher and higher the more I was there, away from her. I cried myself to sleep thinking and thinking about my mom and being home. Mentally and physically I was drained. I felt my happiness being stripped away, every minute and second and millisecond I was feeling worse. All I wanted was to go home. The next day I was still messed up mentally, physically, and emotionally. I woke up early to go to breakfast and find Ms Jackman, who said I was to keep the key for the last two days left in China. At breakfast I felt so much disrespect and hurt from my roommate. I said something to her when it was me, her and another girl talking, and she said, "Do not talk to me." I felt hurt. It felt like a kick in the stomach. I didn't really talk to anyone after that room key problem. I stayed to myself until it was time to leave. The day went by and then I remembered the next day was a great day. Time to go back home. Back to my mom.

Words can't describe how much I missed her. I just wanted to hug her and see her face-to-face. After a three hour plane ride to Tokyo to transfer, we were back on the plane returning to New York City. Thirteen hours apart was finally gonna end. Finally. We landed.

Being back in New York was amazing. I can finally say I've traveled across the world. To a different time zone. To a place outside my comfort zone. When I saw my mom I couldn't help but smile so hard and big. It felt amazing to hold her and look to her for reassurance, I'm amazing now. Seeing you, I'm good. Ms. Jackman gave me and Mom my passport and I headed home. I got home and was greeted to a welcome home sign from my cousin on a shoe box cover. It was so sweet and made me so happy. Being home felt weird at first and I don't know why. I guess being in a different country for so long impacted me. Going to China impacted me for better and for worse. Better because I learned so much. I learned about a different culture and saw so many different things that I never saw in New York, and learned that I shouldn't let people see me at my weakest. It's important that I show that I'm strong on the outside even though on the inside I want to break down. I learned it that it's best to cry in the time of privacy and when you are alone. What was for the worst? People had to see me when I was at my lowest and it was hard to enjoy myself with my mom not being there and I showed my pain and hurt. But I was young then and I've learned a lot since then. I know when to keep a brave face, when to cry, and who to cry to. It's important to show that I can be tough. But I am human and sometimes I show my weakness. Being who I was four years ago when I had my China experience has helped me grow to who I am today.

CHEIKH HAMALAH GUEYE

MY WORST YEAR

Coming from France to the United States was one of my best experiences because it was the first time I flew in a plane. Simultaneously, it was also one of my worst experiences because I left the country that I called home. I immigrated to United States from France on my birthday: June 10, 2014. I travelled with my mother and my two young sisters. My father arrived three years earlier because he had already found a job.

My name is Cheikh, pronounced like "shake." I love soccer; it's my favorite sport. I enjoy playing with my friends in the park. Back home in France, I had two friends with whom I enjoyed playing: Isa and Hussein. I have known them since I was young. Our favorite days to hang out were Friday and Sunday nights. I miss them dearly. Also, there was a beautiful girl who I've been dating for approximately two years who I miss; her name is Matou. The things that I miss most about her are her intelligence and kindness. Aside from missing Isa, Hussein, Matou, and France, I've come to enjoy being in America, a great country with lots of opportunity. The one void that maybe one day will be filled is that I might make good friends here, too.

Traditionally summer is the time to have fun, but my first summer in the U.S was horrible. I didn't have any friends to hang out with. Oh, I forgot to tell you this one thing: I DIDN'T SPEAK ENGLISH, which made it difficult to understand people. Sometimes I'd go to the park with my father, but I was too scared to talk to other kids. So, one day my father made a deal with me. He said, "If you go and ask one kid if you can play with him, I'll buy you a bike."

I was really mad because I wanted the bike and he wouldn't buy it until I'd agree to the deal. I agreed. I walked right up to one boy who was equivalent in height and said, "Est-ce que tu veux jouer avec moi?"

He looked at me and said, "WHAT?" I didn't respond. I just walked away, dejected. Luckily, on other days I had some young cousins who I would spend time with. They didn't live near me, but that was the only time I recall having fun that whole summer.

The summer passed so slowly; before I knew it autumn had arrived, which I wasn't ready for. "Wait, we are in September already? God. School opens this month and I didn't allocate adequate time during the summer teaching myself some English. The least I could have done was learn how to introduce myself to school folk," I said to myself. I worried that since my English speaking ability was very limited that I wasn't going to be able to communicate with people or make friends.

One day in mid-September I was in my bed having a beautiful dream. My father walked into my room and woke me up. He said, "Get up! Today is your first day of school."

I replied, "What? First day of school already? I think you need to check the calendar."

He looked at me and said, "Just get up, you're going to be late." I got up and started getting ready for school.

The school I was to attend wasn't far from where I lived. When I arrived into the school building, I looked right and left, not knowing where to go. I waited until everyone went inside their classes. Since I was by myself in the hallway, the the principal came up to me and asked, "Do you know where your classes are?"

I replied, "Je ne sais pas." He asked my name, looked at my schedule, and showed me my class. Walking into class and not knowing anyone was very awkward in itself. The awkwardness was heightened when I couldn't even find a place to sit. Again, I waited until everyone took their seats and I took the remaining seat. It seemed like school was getting worse by the minute and I still didn't know anyone.

When I walked into the cafeteria that first day, it was a mess with students running around and food left abandoned on the cafeteria tables. I sampled the food; it didn't taste that great. To get your food, you had to put your student I.D. number in a computer, and I didn't know anything about a student ID number. The lady kept saying, "Put in your I.D. number," and I kept putting in random numbers. I was so confused because back in France we didn't have to go through such a process. After I got my lunch, I didn't know where to sit because everyone was with their friends. I ended up sitting in the corner by myself; the solitude made me wonder if I should eat the food or not because I was afraid that I was gonna get sick. After lunch, I had my English as a Second Language (ESL) class. My first day in that class, I felt like the teacher, Ms. Borcher, was mocking me. She told me to write the letters of the alphabet A-Z and then read it to her for the whole period. I didn't understand what the goal of that was.

We got to the point in the school year where we were doing regular school work and teachers started asking the students questions. I was so scared that the teachers would pick me to answer a question that I started sitting in the back of the class. However, that wasn't a good idea in math class because the teacher had a habit of always asking the students in the back.

It wasn't just school that was making the transition difficult. See, I had two younger annoying sisters: Khadija and Aicha, three and two years of age, respectively. Every day, they would mess up my room while I was at school. When I yelled at them, my father would yell right back at me. So, learning English wasn't my only problem: I was also worried about how to live in this house with my two sisters and maintain my sanity. This posed a challenge as I had to babysit them every weekend, too.

In November I felt like school was getting worse. "Hi,

Cheikh. So are you liking the school so far?" Ms. Borcher asked.

I replied, "Not really, because I still couldn't made any good friends to hang out with." "Don't worry, everything will be fine. But for now you need to concentrate on learning English."

One day, I was sitting in my ESL class reading a book and a young lady walked in. Ms. Borcher said, "Cheikh, please meet your new partner. Her name is Junette and she just came here from El Salvador."

Like myself, Junette didn't speak English. I was surprised because until then I'd thought that I was the only one who didn't speak English in the school. But you know what I didn't understand? She made a lot of friends by the next day. In class I tried to be friends with her, but she didn't understand me and I didn't understand her. I was so confused about how she made friends! I thought, "Well, maybe it's because she's a girl, or maybe because she's beautiful, or maybe all her new friends speak Spanish." I was just sitting there, asking myself how she could have possibly made friends in her second day of school. So I was once again sitting in the lunchroom, the worst place to be, wondering if I should eat the food or not. Junette walked up, sat down next to me, took her phone out, and went to Google Translate and typed, "Is everything okay?"

I took her phone and typed, "Yes, I am okay. How about you?" After that day we become friends, I mean close friends.

It was December and we had a few months before school would be out for summer recess. I remember the first time my teacher asked, "Cheikh, could you read the second paragraph for me please."

"Hmm, ok," I answered. It was my first time reading something in front of the whole class. My English was getting a little better and I was shaking so much, but I read it anyway. The next thing I knew everyone was applauding me. I was surprised. "Today is a new day," I said.

I started participating in class. I also started talking to two girls who sat behind me. However, it turned out that they were a distraction to my studies. They started throwing papers at me, then when I threw paper back at them they got mad and told the teacher. The whole class looked at me. I was so scared because I couldn't defend myself. One student who sat on my right side said something to me and everyone started laughing. I didn't know what he said. He looked at me again, but this time I understood what he said. While looking at me, he said, "You crazy." I didn't do anything to him, and he still called me crazy. I looked at him in a very angry way and told him to shut up. With the F word added.

"Cheikh, go to the main office," the teacher said. I proceeded to the main office. One of my teachers was there and she asked me what happened. I took my phone out and translated everything that happened in English. They called my father and he came to pick me up after school.

"Are you okay" he asked.

"Yeah, I am fine, but I just wanna go back home to my old friends and family. I hate it here," I replied.

"Son, just relax and give yourself some time. One day everything will be fine, I promise." He calmed me down by taking me to McDonald's, which we don't usually eat.

Following Christmas break my schedule changed. I deemed this to be a good thing, as I was placed with new classmates who were much nicer people. My day got way worse when they gave us report cards and I found out that I failed the first term. After school, I kept wondering if I should give the report card to my father or not. And Junette just walked toward me and snatched my report card out of my hand and said, "Wow, very good. I failed, too, but at least I got 60 overall average. You got a 58. What were you doing the whole term?"

Then I said, "Yeah, I really messed up this term, but I promise you I will pass the next term. Now can I have my paper?"

"No," she said. I kept getting closer to her to try to get my paper, but she kept refusing to give it to me. I gave her a kiss and she looked at me and said, "Maybe we could be more than friends if you pass the second term," and then she walked away. And no, we didn't use Google translate, if you were wondering. Our English was really getting better! I couldn't believe that I understood English so quickly. I knew that I didn't do anything in the first term, so I decided to stop worrying about making friends and concentrate on my studies. I told my father that I needed weekend classes at the library. I worked really hard in the whole second term. Every day, Junette and I stayed after school with our ESL teacher, learning writing, practicing reading, or sometimes playing chess. Ms. Borcher was the best teacher I ever had. She helped me with everything that I needed help with; she wasn't only a teacher to me, but she was also my friend.

Three months later we got our second term report card. I passed with a 68! I was so excited! I went looking for Junette, and when I found her I asked, "So, how was your report card?" She gave me her report card; she passed with a 72. "Wow, you're so smart," I said.

"Thanks. So, what's your overall average?"

"I got a 68. That's bad, right?"

"What do you mean, it's bad? You passed! Come on, give me a hug."

"So now are we still friends, or more then friends?"

"Whatever you want to go with," she said. And I went for the kiss again. My life changed after that day because I stopped worrying about friends. She wasn't only my girlfriend, she was also my helper. We read books and did homework together every lunch period and after school. I learned a lot of things from her. She always wanted to know why I didn't want to make friends.

I told her, "Why do I need friends when I have you?" From that day through the end of that school year, she was the only person that I hung out with.

MICHELLE BERTRAND

FINDING MY VOICE

I think part, if not most, of me has always felt this sadness that I could never shake off. No matter where I was or who I was with, I just never felt joy or happiness. I got pretty good at pretending though. Nobody wanted to be friends with the "sad kid" that I was at 4, at 10, at 16, and so on. So I created a facade. The facade was "happy me," because I knew there was no true medicine for this melancholy.

Daycares and pre-school were the hardest. Growing up, I never wanted to play with other kids. I didn't want any interaction, period. I hated when people touched me, or got too loud or too close. I had this uncontrollable fear of speaking to anyone who wasn't a family member and never wanted my mother to leave me whenever she dropped me off at school. As a child I also developed a number of phobias and fears that followed me into adulthood that I am still managing today. One day, my mother came to pick me up from daycare and saw that I was playing in a corner alone. She knew from there that there was something wrong with me. She suspected that I might have been autistic; however, being a product of her generation she saw that I was still able to somewhat function like a "normal" child and did nothing about it. I guess that at the time there was little to no information easily accessible on high functioning autism.

From elementary school to middle school I was bullied. It was awful. I was really quiet and I enjoyed being by myself even though I had friends. I never spoke up about what was happening because I was afraid of my own voice; I was afraid to have a voice. I went home crying nearly every day. I was bullied by bullies and I was even bullied by people who were supposed to be friends. They'd find anything to make fun of but me; my acne was always their favorite. It eventually made me hate my face. My insecurities had become so crippling that I wouldn't let anyone pictures and if I took school pictures I would rip them all up before anyone in my family could see one. I believe around fifth grade was the time I first began to harbor suicidal thoughts and seventh grade was my first suicide attempt. It happened after I was molested by a friend of my father's. My father still doesn't know, and probably never will.

In the winter of 2010 my mother was diagnosed with breast cancer. At the time I was a sophomore in high school. On April 24, 2013, she passed away, just a month before her birthday and two months before my graduation from high school. From the moment my mother was diagnosed, and up until her death, I watched her suffer almost every day as her body deteriorated in front of my eyes. My mother's health took a major toll on my mental health to the point where I tried to take my own life three days prior to her death.

I tried to cope with my mother's passing by getting really busy. I started college immediately, which I learned was a mistake. I failed out of college my first semester. I went back and tried another semester in hopes of getting my grades back on track. My dream was to go back to a senior college but I realized I hadn't taken time off to heal. The grief hit me hard and made it impossible for me to focus or even attend class most days. I was diagnosed with MDD (Major Depressive Disorder) and anxiety. No one ever tells you what that truly means. Depression is more than just feeling sad all the time. Depression causes people to sometimes stay in bed all day, overeat, or (like in my case) hardly eat anything. People with depression sometimes avoid leaving the house, skip showers, have a constant feeling of guilt, and sometimes lose interest in activities that they used to enjoy. I never told anyone outside of my family but that's how I spent almost every single day from the ending of 2013 to the beginning of

2017. Losing my mother left a permanent hole in my heart.

One night after crying and crying for hours, I decided I couldn't take it anymore. I either had to find a way to deal with this abundance of pain that I had in me or I would end up dead by my own hands and those thoughts had always scared me. So I started free writing until my emotions became words and then kept writing until my words began to make sense. Through all that writing what I came up with was a pilot to a screenplay. The screenplay is helping me to both express myself and to tell my story, which I think is very important. I had always used writing as an outlet for my emotions, whether the writing was poetry, stories, etc. but after my mom died it was hard for me to write anything.

I wish I could say that since that night my life has done a total 180 and I am no longer depressed, but I can't. However, what I can say is that writing has saved me and continues to save me every day. It is the light at the end of my darkest tunnels. I realized that night that I want my writing to not only reflect my life and my experiences, but the life and the experiences of every young person of color who goes through unimaginable things every day. I believe that representation is vital and it is extremely important that children of color see and read things that remind them of themselves or someone they know. So I guess through my sadness I found my calling.

DARK BEAUTY

Dear black woman
You are so beautiful
In every single way
From head to toe
And with every word you say
Black woman
Your divine feminine grace
Lingers in the minds
Of anyone who gets to know you
If they dare and if you may
Your energy leaves them ruminating
Even if only offered a little taste
For your true beauty derives
From a different kind of place
From the lonely nights you've cried
And your never ending journey to the other side
It comes from the dark days you wished you weren't alive
The past trauma
That had deeply rooted itself inside
The pain was just some of
The reasons you were asking God why
Why you were chosen for this burden
Because it was all too much
And the future seemed uncertain
Not knowing those were the times
The devil was creepin, really lurkin
Yet somehow you managed
You were broken
But you were not damaged
Black woman
Through your pain and your journey of healing
You have gained many things
Like your empathy

Your understanding
How you love endlessly
And the way you've become so caring
Black woman
You are warm, sweet, soft
Gentle yet strong
Shining as bright as the sun
Black woman, black women
You are as beautiful as they come

CYCLES

Am I a fool?
To think I'd truly be loved by someone like you
To think that you'd want the home I built within me
A home where only you have the key
To think that just me would be
Enough for you when who I am isn't even enough for anybody
My mirror projects an image of a person I don't recognize
I don't see . . . me
Am I my mother, like the others? Another
Woman begging to be loved
Thinking back on my father's acts
The lies the way he'd womanize and ignore my mother's cries
Those many nights my mother spent alone
In the room they both shared in our home
Intimacy was something he lacked
And lack of affection is all she'd ever known
Because her mother too loved a man
Whose heart was also made of stone
She'd been married off at 18
Made to bear children
Life quickly became lull, stilled in
As dreams began to fade, the joy followed
Then the laughter
'Til the love finally disappeared shortly after
Now here we are
And it all seems a bit familiar
The past meeting the present
Time begins to intertwine
The present becoming the past
As I simply come to find
Nothing truly ever lasts
I should've paid attention to the signs

ABOUT THE WRITERS

Annalise Thomas

Annalise Thomas attends Brooklyn Generation School located in the South Shore campus in Brooklyn, New York. She was born in Guyana but later moved to Brooklyn, New York at the age of six with her single working mother. She attended P.S. 235 and also the Middle School for Marketing and Legal Studies, both located in Brooklyn. During the years she attended the Middle School for Marketing and Legal Studies she invested her after school time developing her interest in dance and step with the Student Athlete Scholarship Foundation. In her current high school she is a member of Brooklyn College TRIO and serves as a Youth Leader.

Amalaa Joseph

Amalaa Joseph is a tenth grade student at Brooklyn Generation School in the South Shore Campus. So far in her two wonderful years of high school, she's been exposed to many great opportunities and privileges. She has participated in college tours to various campuses including Daemen College, Cornell University, Manhattanville College, and SUNY Cortland. She has also become a Youth Leader in her school. Amalaa thanks her mom for being her number one support system and helping her be the best she can be, pushing her to keep striving and taking part in all the opportunities that come her way.

Ar'Maunie Blalock

Ar'Maunie Blalock, a freshman at Brooklyn Generation School, is originally from Youngstown, Ohio. She lived there until the end of fourth grade. After her fourth grade year, she moved with her family to Atlanta, Georgia where she lived until the end of her seventh grade year. When her father was diagnosed with cancer her family moved to New York so he could obtain treatment. For her eighth grade year, she was homeschooled and she was initially reluctant to leave the comforts of home to attend public school. She's thrilled that she gave public school a chance because of all the wonderful experiences she's had in her freshman year. These experiences include becoming a Youth Leader, going on college trips, and being introduced to many teenagers and adults that she loves being around. In 2018, Ar'Maunie hopes to be engaged in the Arthur Ashe Institute for Urban Health which will help her to pursue her dream medical career.

Brooke-Lynn Bascombe

Brooke-Lynn Bascombe is a 16 years old student born in November 2001. She currently attends Brooklyn Generation School and will graduate in 2019. Aside from traditional school work, she is a youth leader in the College Prep Academy, an AVID student, a TRIO student, and is taking a College Now class at Brooklyn College. In college Brooke Lynn plans to major in tourism and hospitality, travel and see the world.

Cheikh Hamalah Gueye

Cheikh Hamalah Gueye was born in June 2001, in Paris, France. His family and friends describe him as affectionate, amiable and compassionate. He lives in a home with both parents and six younger siblings; three brothers and three sisters. He attended school at Marymount International School in Paris. On his fourteenth birthday, Cheikh moved to the United States.

He currently attends Brooklyn Generation School and is a Youth Leader in the school's College Prep Academy, a student at the Arthur Ashe Institute for Urban Health, and a member of row team for Row New York. He has taken College Now classes at Brooklyn College and is a former member of the South Shore soccer team. Soccer is his favorite sport; he loves both watching and playing. He began taking acting lessons at the age of eleven. His big dream is to become an actor and pursue a career on the big screen.

Daniel Lewis

Daniel Lewis lived most of his life in Kingston, Jamaica surrounded by the love of his family: his mother Denise, sister Janelle, maternal grandmother Elaine, and paternal grandmother Gloria. At an early age Daniel was fascinated by airplanes and, as he gazed in the sky, could easily identify the type of airplane as they flew overhead. Daniel graduated as valedictorian, class of 2015 from Brooklyn Generation School. He is pursuing a professional pilot license while majoring in aviation management and business management at SUNY Farmingdale, with an expected graduation date of May 2020.

Keston Hall

Keston is a high school student from Brooklyn, New York who loves music and video games. He states that his father's teachings are what have given him the desire to succeed in life. His father showed him the real world but allowed him to discover some things on his own. In the future he wants to own his own business. Realizing that he has many years to decide on a career, Keston takes advantage of all opportunities that come his way. He is a participant in the Arthur Ashe Bridge Academy and plans on taking college classes this summer at Long Island University, Brooklyn campus.

Ivancile Jules

Ivancile is a standout athlete at the South Shore Campus and a diligent student in Brooklyn Generation High School. He has participated in a great many extracurricular activities that his school has provided, including AVID, Brooklyn College TRIO, serving as a Youth Leader with the College Prep Academy, and competing in track & field and football. He believes all these opportunities have shaped him into the well-developed young man he is today. He also believes not just in himself, but that there is greatness in everyone and that it is a person's responsibility to make a self-conscious decision to harness their individual greatness. Throughout his high school career, he continues to be known for receiving good grades, building bonds with staff members and peers and showing strong leadership capabilities. For these reasons he is respected by staff and peers. In the near future he hopes to become licensed as a Certified Public Accountant and train to become a professional athlete.

Michelle Rose Alta-Grace Bertrand

Michelle Rose Alta-Grace Bertrand was born in Brooklyn, NY in February 1995 to Lourdes Toussaint (May 25, 1964- April 24, 2013), a hairdresser/salon owner, and Robinson Bertand, a police officer for the state of Georgia. As a child, Michelle attended St. Vincent Ferrer school in Brooklyn and took ballet lessons at Francine's dance studio. Growing up, Michelle was a quiet child who spent most of her time writing poetry and short stories. She used writing as an outlet to express personal emotions and to also reflect on the world around her. Michelle is currently a youth advocate for the Mental Health Association of New York City, where she works with "at-risk youth". She is an aspiring writer/ actress who is a strong believer in representation and hopes to someday make a difference through her art.

Neika Victor

Neika Victor, a current high school junior at Brooklyn Generation School, is one of the original Youth Leaders in the school's College Prep Academy and also a scholar at the Arthur Ashe Institute for Urban Health. Additionally, she is an AVID student, a member of the Brooklyn College TRIO program and is currently enrolled in a Speech Communication class through College Now at Brooklyn College. She enjoys reading and writing poetry. Neika believes that poetry is an important form of art that can be used to express yourself.

Raquel Gracien
Raquel Gracien is 16-year-old African-American girl in her third year at Brooklyn Generation High School. Raquel was born and raised in Brooklyn. She comes from a big family and has lived with her mom, siblings, cousins and aunt. She is a go-getter, if she wants something she'll strive to complete the goal. She is also a person that speaks her mind and doesn't care what others say or think about her. She has always set high expectations for herself. Raquel is a Youth Leader for the Brooklyn Generation Community and a Brooklyn College TRIO member. Besides that, she is currently taking not only SAT prep but Regents prep and a Psychology course for the College-Now program at Brooklyn College.

Rose Landa Solon
Rose Landa Solon is an immigrant from Haiti, she came to New York on July 17, 2016. She lives in Brooklyn with her lovely family, her encouraging mom (Roselie Massenat), her strong dad (Prophane Solon) and also her siblings (Vedeline, Stephanie, Genite, Elitchama, Stephenson, Dawens). Rose Landa is a Christian, an eleventh grader at Brooklyn Generation School, a member of Brooklyn College Trio, and she is also a Youth leader in her school. Her family and friends see her as affectionate, compassionate, helpful, and wise. She has written poetry in French, English and Creole. She also participates in Urban Arts Partnership's dance program at BGS.

Samoya Salmon
Samoya Salmon is a student of Brooklyn Generation School, a student athlete and a Youth Leader at the school. Samoya was born in the Caribbean, she's 16 years old and currently lives with her mom in Brooklyn, New York. She's

an excellent student who strives to do her best in anything she does.

Sherell Henry

Sherell Henry is a young black woman living in a society that teaches and shapes children of color to believe that they cannot achieve the impossible because they are not white. Sherell was born at Brookdale Hospital and spent her early childhood living with her father's aunt in Trinidad. At the age of eight Sherell moved to New York. Currently she attends Brooklyn Generation School. She is also a youth leader working with other students. She loves learning about the universe and the planets. She enjoys mathematics and being able to develop codes to carry out a function within a device. She wants to be able to change the world and create a better future for Black kids, giving children of color who were denied the opportunity to show their talent another chance.

Steven Gomez

Stephen Gomez is a senior at Brooklyn Generation School. During his years in high school he didn't find his calling until late in his sophomore year. At that time he became a Youth Leader in College Prep Academy and realized almost instantly that he enjoyed helping others. During the process of helping others he learned that he really wanted to go to college. In the Fall of 2018 he will be a freshman at SUNY Tompkins Cortland Community College.

Telena Smith

Telena Smith was born in Georgetown, Guyana to Rawle and Taundy Smith in September, 1999. She migrated to Brooklyn, New York at a young age in pursuit of education. Telena graduated from Brooklyn Generation School where she took advantage of the many academic and social activities offered to her; Arthur Ashe Institute for Urban Health, Brooklyn College TRIO, Brooklyn College College

Now, Medgar Evers College Now, Monroe Jumpstart, STEP (Science Technology Entry Program) at DownState, Columbia C.A.S.H (College Awareness Symbolizes Hope), Urban Arts Partnership, and Brooklyn Generation School College Prep Academy. She was one of the founding members of the Brooklyn Generation School Youth Leaders. Telena currently attends Daemen College on a full scholarship and completed her first semester on the Dean's List. While she has not declared a major she is leaning towards a career as an occupational therapist.

Made in the USA
Columbia, SC
30 March 2018